# WORKING
# AS ONE BODY

The Report
of the Archbishops' Commission
on the Organisation
of the Church of England

# WORKING
# AS ONE BODY

The Report
of the Archbishops' Commission
on the Organisation
of the Church of England

CHURCH HOUSE PUBLISHING
Church House, Great Smith Street, London SW1P 3NZ

ISBN 0 7151 3763 8

Published 1995 by Church House Publishing

© *The Central Board of Finance of the Church of England 1995*

Cover design by Leigh Hurlock

Printed in England by the University Printing House, Cambridge

# Contents

# Foreword by the Archbishops

Bishop Michael Turnbull and his colleagues were invited to recommend ways of strengthening the effectiveness of the Church's central policy-making and resource direction machinery. They were encouraged not to shrink from radical ideas. Their report is forthright about the challenges which face the Church; much needs to be changed if the Church is to work effectively as one body. Most of the work of the Church of England is, as the report emphasises, carried out in the dioceses and parishes, but there are important functions which can only be carried out effectively at a national level.

This report sets out a clear way forward which we believe would enable the Church to be better equipped for the challenges of the next millennium. The broad thrust of its overall conclusion, that there should be a new mechanism for securing coherence in the work of the Church of England at the national level, is one which we support.

The report should now be considered fully at all levels within and outside the Church and we warmly encourage wide debate on it. We shall listen carefully to all the views expressed in due course through the General Synod and by other means. We then need to move purposefully to implement what is decided upon, in order to avoid prolonged uncertainty. Our priority must be to use whatever new structures emerge for advancing the mission and ministry of the Church to the nation.

We are most grateful to Bishop Michael and his colleagues for the speed and thoroughness with which they have worked. We hope this report will be given the careful and prayerful consideration which it deserves.


+ George Cantuar:
+ John Ebor:

August 1995

# Chairman's Preface

The Archbishop of Canterbury and the Archbishop of York presented me and my colleagues on the Commission with a tremendous challenge when they invited us to review the central policy-making and resource direction machinery of the Church of England. They put together a Commission comprising people of very wide experience from within the Church and the public and private sectors. The membership and background to the Commission's work are set out in appendix A. We have enjoyed intellectual and personal companionship of a high order in our work and in praying and worshipping together.

We decided at the outset that we were willing if necessary to be very radical. In looking at the organisational arrangements at the centre we considered a wide variety of options. That process of questioning and of theological discussion brought home to us the fundamental ecclesiological significance of the Anglican model which combines episcopal leadership with synodical governance. It became our common purpose – and our shared commitment – to develop organisational arrangements which would enable those elements to work vigorously and healthily for the good of the Church as a whole.

We believe our proposals are both theologically sound and practically based. The structural changes we propose, and the cultural changes we are convinced the Church must embrace, will enable policy to be made in a more purposeful manner and allow the Church to make proper arrangements for the effective use of its resources.

We value and admire the commitment and dedication with which office holders and staff in the central institutions of the Church seek to serve the Church as a whole. Our recommendations imply no criticism whatsoever of individuals. The problems and shortcomings lie with structures and systems rather than people.

We have worked swiftly, deeply conscious of the weight of expectation which rests upon our report. We believe the changes we propose are both urgent and necessary. This is why we have included in appendix B a draft Measure to illustrate how they might be given a statutory basis.

On a personal note I cannot praise too highly the commitment of every member of the Commission to an intensely demanding task. All members put in long hours and much work was willingly done in small groups between meetings.

We were fortunate to have the Bishop of Ely as Theological Adviser and the experience and skills of our Assessors. The Secretariat of Janet Lewis-Jones, Mark Humphriss and Ronnie Ferguson provided tremendous support. Their organisational and drafting skills were a quite indispensable part of the process.

Our report is unanimous. We signed it in the context of a shared Eucharist. We feel it could introduce a new era of openness, optimism and vigour in the Church and hope it will be received in that spirit.

+ Michael Dunelm:

26 July 1995

# 1

# The organisation of the Church in the light of the gifts of God

## The Commission's approach

1.1    The Church of England is part of the one, holy, catholic and apostolic Church. The Archbishops' Commission made this its starting point: the understanding that the Church is an integral part of the mystery of God's reconciling work in his world, and an embodiment of the presence of God in his world. We were asked to make recommendations about the life not of a business but of a Church in the Anglican tradition, and the conclusions at which we arrived are, we believe, wholly consistent with that tradition. It combines leadership by bishops with governance by synods representing bishops, clergy and laity. It avoids a large, centralised bureaucracy because it regards leadership as essentially the enablement of life and work in the dioceses, parishes and other spheres of Christian discipleship.

1.2    The Anglican tradition calls for every member of the Church to share responsibility. All must work together as one body, for all have a part to play in response to Christ's call in bearing witness to Christ, in the making of policies in the cause of Christ and in the provision of the resources needed to put those policies into effect. Whether or not we are ordained leaders, or elected to serve on synods or committees, we all have our different contributions to make in response to Christ's call. These contributions are our compelling duties. Moreover, we all need to have a right relationship with those who discharge the responsibilities of leadership on behalf of the whole Church. We need to know that those who have been called to these responsibilities are properly accountable but we also need to feel able to trust them to use their own gifts faithfully in the furtherance of the gospel and the service of the Church. All this is taught to us by our Anglican tradition.

1.3    At the same time we have drawn upon the gifts, insights and wisdom of Church people with substantial experience of non-ecclesiastical organisations. In this way a dialogue has built up between Christian theology and organisational theory, as we have reflected on such matters as clarity of vision, coherence, effectiveness, responsibility and processes of change within the life of the Church. In the development of our thinking we have frequently found ourselves making explicit ways of working together which have long been implicit in the life of the Church of England. We make no apology therefore for beginning our report with chapters which some may think surprisingly theoretical or theological. We have been determined to attempt the task of providing a sound intellectual and spiritual basis for the national structures of the Church of England in its service to the nation as a whole. That is reflected in the structure of our report: chapters 1 and 2 set out the insights on which we have drawn in considering the nature and purpose of the mechanisms we describe in the remaining chapters.

## The polity of the Church

1.4    The Commission found itself, in effect, reflecting on the 'polity' of the Church. Polity, in this sense, means 'civil organisation or order' (OED). We were doing nothing new. In *The Laws of Ecclesiastical Polity*, published at the end of the sixteenth century, the Anglican theologian Richard Hooker attempted to show how God's own order in creation and redemption should be reflected in the way the Church of England was governed. His book was written under the pressure of particular historical conditions and controversies, which have greatly changed. But the effort to understand how the people of God combine and work together to do God's work in the world, with greater insight, persistence and effectiveness, is not a novelty for Anglicans and we discovered important continuities with our tradition as well as new challenges to meet.

1.5    We oriented ourselves by reference to the most fundamental truths. The life of the Church, since it is a consequence of God's love for humanity, must be relational and personal. St Paul, who articulated the image of the Church as being like a body with many limbs and organs, affirms that we are Christ's body and that that body is held together and built up by love. The Church has been brought into being by the love of God for humanity. God loved the world so much that he gave his only Son. The Church is the body of those who believe in the Son, and, as his bride, is the object of the Son's own love. We live out of the resources which God in his love has promised and given, by the Holy Spirit shed abroad in the hearts of the faithful.

1.6    The life of the Church, in a rich and yet mysterious way, is thus utterly trinitarian in its ground, being and hope. We worship the one

God, Father, Son and Holy Spirit. As the people of the new covenant, the Church is radically dependent upon the outpouring of the Holy Spirit, a gift who inspires our worship and whose giving is the guarantee of a still greater inheritance to come. The Church is gathered together in gratitude for the justifying and reconciling activity of the Son of God, who gave himself as a sacrifice for the sin of the whole world, and who rose again so that all might have access to the Father through him. But the Church is also firmly part of God's good creation, an assembly of men and women of varying gifts and abilities, who love and support one another through all the joys and difficulties of their daily lives. Thus the Church comes to be both 'a society and a society supernatural' (Richard Hooker, *Laws* I, xv, 2).

1.7    The fundamental task and aims of the Church of England are those of the one, holy, catholic and apostolic Church. They are not invented or researched by theologians or commissions of enquiry. They are given by divine commission. There is a variety of ways in which the Church's sense of being sent is expressed in the New Testament. It is to go to all nations and make them disciples of the Lord. His followers are sent by Christ into the world, as he was sent by the Father into the world. God has entrusted the Church's ministers with the task of being his ambassadors, and makes his appeal for reconciliation through them. As the Church reflected on this mission it formulated four classic 'marks' or 'attributes' which ought to characterise its life at all times and in all places. It is to be *one*, that is to proclaim and to embody the reconciliation of all things in Christ; to be *holy*, to have about it the marks of the sanctifying presence of the Holy Spirit; to be *catholic*, that is to be, as Christ is, for all people, at all times, in all places; and to be *apostolic*, to witness to the authentic and liberating gospel as taught by the apostles.

1.8    Together with all these marks goes a concealed presupposition, that the Church must be a learning community. It can manifest none of the four attributes unless Christians corporately go to school with Christ, are nourished by teaching and the sacraments, and grow up into his likeness. Thus the Church is a school in which the gift of teaching is acknowledged, but in which all the teachers are themselves pupils, enjoying mutuality of encouragement and correction.

1.9    Although we might rightly say that, in this way, the *aims* of the Church of England have already been given to it, it has continually to formulate and reformulate its specific *objectives* with a view to their being consistent with these fundamental aims and also appropriate and relevant to the conditions of our land in our time. The gospel has to be proclaimed afresh in each generation. New challenges and opportunities constantly arise; new threats have to be resisted. The exigencies of history and sheer human laziness and complacency require that the Church should ask itself searching questions about the faithfulness and effectiveness of its witness. The questions which inevitably arise are characteristically both theological and practical. To speak of the Church's 'direction' and 'effectiveness' (as do the terms of our enquiry) is to imply a grasp upon the mission which God has given to the Church; but at the same time it demands a critical and imaginative insight into current failures and future possibilities. What is asked of the Church at this particular moment is a combination of fidelity and expertise of various kinds in the formulation of its current objectives.

## The theology of gracious gift

1.10    What underlies the way we have gone about our present task in this Commission is a theology of gracious gift; that is to say, we are convinced that God in his goodness has already given to the Church the resources it needs to be God's people, and to live and work to his praise and glory. The most fundamental resource is that of a common fellowship or sharing in the Holy Spirit, which we enjoy as members together of the body of Christ. Membership is given at baptism, and from baptism derives the radical equality of status enjoyed by all the baptised. In the body of Christ all are sinners redeemed by grace. Within this body the one Spirit gives a variety of gifts. All these gifts are to be used in humility and love, with attentiveness to the gifts and interests of others, and with the goal of building up the whole body, and increasing its effectiveness.

1.11    The early Christian communities saw themselves as a special and distinct form of corporate existence. They spoke of themselves as a people or nation, but one without any racial or social qualifications. They were ridiculed as a 'third race', neither Greek nor barbarian. Much of their distinctiveness consisted in the quality of their personal relationships, and their at least partial re-ordering of systems of status and rank, based on conversion to Christ and baptism. The letters of the New Testament were written to, and reflect the struggles of, the new communities to realise this vision in a complex and hostile environment.

1.12    Because the work of Christ was itself the reconciliation of humanity (Colossians 1.20) there is, from the first, strong evidence of concern for the unity of the communities, both in their internal relationships, and in their interrelationships. St Paul, for example, writes of his anxiety for the continuity of preaching and teaching the authentic gospel, and for the effectiveness of the united witness of the Church to the gospel of reconciliation. God has given the Church various gifts, to be used in love for the good of the whole, including the gift of leadership. St Paul's own ministry of leadership is itself God-given for the same purpose.

1.13    Leadership entails a ministry of *episcope,* exercised in a variety of functions within a local church which, as a whole, is apostolic. Among the tasks of the minister with oversight are 'leadership in mission; in the ministry of the word and sacraments; in worship, prayer and praise; in guardianship of the faith; in the declaration of the forgiveness of sins to those who turn to God in repentance and faith; in discipline; and the minister has had special responsibilities in commissioning for ministry in the Church on behalf of the community' (*Apostolicity and Succession: A House of Bishops Occasional Paper,* GS Misc. 432, 1994, p 17). An effective carrying out of these many tasks involves delegation and sharing (*Episcopal Ministry: The Report of the Archbishops' Group on the Episcopate,* GS 944, 1990, pp 175-180). But *episcope* (literally 'oversight') involves preserving a synoptic vision of the whole, together with responsibilities for ensuring the co-ordination of each aspect of the mission of the Church.

1.14    A principal purpose of what we now recognise as a special or 'ordained' ministry is to serve the continuity and effectiveness of witness to the gospel of Jesus Christ. This ministry has arisen by stages out of what St Paul spoke of as the ministries of apostles, prophets, teachers and many others. The ordained ministry of deacons, priests and bishops performs for our time the task of leadership which St Paul, and later St Timothy, performed for theirs, in serving, in teaching, encouraging, nurturing, guiding, co-ordinating and if necessary disciplining the exercise of the manifold gifts of the whole people of God.

1.15    It is in this way that we come to understand a variety of levels on which the God-given mission of the Church is carried out. To be the people of God means to live in a certain quality of personal, face-to-face relationships, embodying God's reconciliation of all things in Christ, living in the light of God's justice, forgiveness and new life. It is through the witness of the Church to the reality of that new life that the attractiveness of the gospel becomes apparent. At the same time care has to be taken to preserve the continuity of that witness across time, and its coherence and effectiveness in different places. Integral to, and serving the level of, the inter-personal, are the levels of the local, regional or national. From very early times the office of the bishop was seen as serving both of these functions, preserving continuity and nurturing the effectiveness of the mission of the Church. But that office could only achieve its purposes in reciprocal relationship to the level of the personal, face-to-face life of the communities. In modern language, the office of the bishop is at once personal (a God-given personal responsibility), collegial (a responsibility to be exercised together with those with whom the bishop shares the task of oversight) and communal (that is, in unbreakable relationship to the whole community of the baptised).

1.16    Thus the Church has developed its own distinctive structures and polity on the basis of its divine commission and self-understanding. It is not a democracy, governed by elected representatives responsible solely to its electorate; nor is it a line-management hierarchy, distributing specific powers and responsibility on a command-obedience model. So far as status is concerned, there is none higher than that of being baptised into Christ. The basis of the Church's polity can only be that of the recognition of the many diverse gifts graciously given to God's people, to be used co-operatively to his glory and for the salvation of humanity.

1.17    The specific tasks of those who have received the gift of episcopal ordination among the people of God have varied across the centuries, and in different cultures. Societies develop their own patterns of leadership with which they feel content, and within those societies the authority accorded to leadership within the Church has varied, as have safeguards against its abuse. At the Reformation the Church of England took pains to continue the threefold orders it had inherited from ancient times. At the same time it gave to the laity of the Church increased access to the Scriptures and to the liturgy in their own tongue, and to a place and voice in the Church's polity through the role of the Sovereign-in-Parliament. The diocese remained the principal unit of the Church, because of the bishop's responsibility to oversee the Church's mission and the ministry of word and sacrament in that specific place.

1.18    The development of synodical government in the Anglican community is a long story to which there are many strands. A brief account is given in chapter 6 (see paragraph 6.9ff). The structures have gradually evolved in response to the conditions, perceived needs and secular models of the day. But a consistent thread in the whole history is the idea of leadership by an episcopate which has consulted with, and gained the consent of, both their fellow clergy and the laity. It has antecedents in the so-called conciliarist movement of the fourteenth century, which located the authority of the Church not in the hierarchy exclusively but in the whole body of the faithful united in the sacraments. The conciliar model of the Bishop-in-Synod provides the basis of the Commission's proposals.

1.19   The Churches of the Anglican Communion have come to be spoken of currently as 'episcopally led and synodically governed'. This useful and convenient phrase may, however, tend to conceal the fact that the bishops are part of the synod and that the leadership they give is in and to the whole synodical body. The reason for these developments needs, however, to be explicitly acknowledged. It lies in the theology of gracious gift. Ordination is one of the gifts of the Holy Spirit, who gives liberally to every member of the body. But the task of the Church requires the co-ordination of the many gifts of the Spirit, and a synod is one way in which counsel may be taken and consent sought, and the skills and judgement of the whole people of God may be brought to bear on the issues and challenges of the day.

1.20   A synod is also a way of focusing debate. In this connection we can explicitly recognise the potentially constructive character of dis-agreement and differences of view within the one body. Because there is always the possibility of misunderstanding and error in the fresh procla-mation of the gospel, and because of the new challenges and opportuni-ties which constantly arise, Christians have always engaged in vigorous debate with each other. Providing differences do not harden into fac-tiousness and bitterness, argument with respect has a vital role to play in the life of the Church. The communion of the Holy Spirit is always a dynamic holding of the tensions of this process. As a result clarity about the objectives of the Church within a given culture should never be bought at the cost of a suppression of variety. A synod is one way in which this variety can be made fruitful to the life of the Church.

1.21   All this means that the description and practice of authority in the Church is no easy matter. But it is right to begin with the assertion that all authority and power (the relation of the terms is ambiguous, even in the scriptures) is to be ascribed to God.

1.22   In Jesus' own exercise of his authority and power we see certain crucial features. He uses his power to confront evil and to challenge untruth; he acts not as a domineering force, but in service to his brothers and sisters; he goes out of his way to include those whom society casts out into its margins; he values humility highly and makes himself finally vulnerable.

7

1.23    In the letters of St Paul we see a vivid struggle taking place between what he calls his 'weakness' and his 'strength'. The possibility of the abuse of authority and power is already envisaged within the New Testament churches, and the story of Jesus' rebuke to the disciples for their 'jealous dispute' (Luke 22.24) was preserved as plainly relevant to contemporary conditions.

1.24    A theology of gracious gift does not, however, fail to acknowledge that God has given outstanding skills of leadership to particular individuals. Sometimes these are competences which are fully acknowledged in secular contexts, such as gifts of personality, articulacy, capacity for work, imagination, management and organisational skills or conceptual clarity. Sometimes these are specific to Christian faith, such as godliness, spiritual insight, prayerfulness, humility, infectious joy, a love for souls, evangelistic zeal and so forth. It serves the Church well when those who recognisably have these gifts, whether they are laity or clergy, are brought together to provide a coherent strategy for the Church as a whole.  It does not serve the Church well if those who possess such gifts are treated with jealousy or mistrust. At the same time it is prudent to ensure that the Church is protected from human proneness to mistake the limits of those gifts, or to come to enjoy power over others at the very moment when the gifts are recognised.

1.25    Whereas the natural inclination of those with authority and power may be to protect themselves from criticism, the structures which require consultation make them vulnerable. The same processes may also have the effect of enhancing the collective impact of the whole Church, as a diversity of gifts is brought together in fruitful dialogue, and the authority and power of the co-operating membership is co-ordinated to a given end. It is, therefore, a mistake simply to construe powers as though they stand for necessarily conflicting interest groups, in which more power to one group inevitably implies less power to another. While proper place must be given to a process in which the abuse of power can be recognised and resisted, the Church should encourage those with gifts to use them in service to the whole body, and especially in the interests of those whom society marginalises. In a theology of gracious gift the first words must be gratitude, love, service, humility and trust. In such a way the Church can, in its very structures and processes, embody the mission on which it has been sent. Though Christian wisdom knows the reality of deviousness and self-deception, the Church should not institutionally fetter itself to the expectation of rivalry and mutual suspicion. The wisdom of the Church has been to require consultation between those to whom authority and power has been entrusted and those in relation to whom it is to be exercised. Our recommendations build on this foundation.

# 2

# The mission of the Church and the task of this Commission

## The threefold mission of the local church

2.1    We have set out in the previous chapter how the distinctive communal life of the Church is fundamental to its identity. It is no accident, therefore, that the mission of the Church of England is most clearly and gloriously seen in the parishes. They do not represent the whole of the Church's work but it is true to say that without them the main purpose of the Church would be lost. The structures of the Church must therefore be, and be seen to be, in integral relation to and support of the congregations and parishes in which the distinctive quality of corporate existence comes to expression. When the local, regional or national structures fail in that role the Church is impeded in its mission.

2.2    At each of the meetings of the Commission, we have begun with the following prayer:

> *O God,*
> *in whose sovereign power*
> *rests everything in heaven and earth;*
> *take hold of your Church today*
> *that in the organisation of its work*
> *the use of its resources*
> *and the planning of its strategy*
> *it may serve this nation with humility*
> *witness to your love with boldness*
> *and worship you in holiness;*
> *through Jesus Christ our Lord.   Amen.*

We have thus affirmed that the mission of the Church and the resources to carry it out are a free gift of God's grace. All that we do is under his sovereignty. We have recognised, too, that our response to God's graciousness is threefold – worship, service and witness.

2.3    **Worship** is the response of the creature to the creator and without it our humanity is diminished. Christian worship is radically trinitarian. In the power of the Holy Spirit we respond to a God who has revealed himself – in creation, in history and supremely in the person of Jesus Christ. The traditions of the Church of England include a strong emphasis upon common prayer in liturgical forms giving pre-eminence to scripture as the uniquely inspired witness to God's revelation in Christ. The authorised texts of our liturgies, both the Book of Common Prayer of 1662, and the Alternative Service Book of 1980, share also in the liturgical heritage of western Christianity, and we stand in continuity with the Church of the patristic and medieval periods both directly and through the insights of the Reformation period. The traditions of spirituality, worship and sacramental life are indispensable to the identity of the Church of England. The response that God enables us to make to his grace may be seen in three interconnected aspects, those of worship, service and witness.

2.4    The Canon Law of the Church of England lays upon a bishop the duty to provide a place of worship in every parish, and every parish must provide regular worship in its place of worship, including provision for the regular celebration of the sacraments. The provision of worship in every parish is a requirement which the Church gladly accepts but it has important effects on the organisation of the Church and on the use of its resources. It underlies the fact that the Church of England has to be organised on considerations based on service to the community as a whole and its obligations under God and to the State. For instance, the Church cannot pull out of parishes which do not 'pay' and simply concentrate on 'successful' areas. The provision of Church of England liturgy, ministry and a place of worship for every parish is an accepted part of its mission from which it would not wish to abdicate.

2.5    **Service** to the community is the second aspect of the Church of England's tripartite mission. If worship attempts to fulfil 'You shall love the Lord your God with all your heart . . .', so care and service is a response to the second commandment '. . . and your neighbour as yourself' (Matthew 22.37-39). The two are inseparable. Worship without active love in the world leads to spiritual ghettos. Jesus made it clear by his life and his teaching that worship, teaching and healing were integral to each other. Moreover, he commissioned his disciples to do this not only for individuals but in the context of community: the object is the establishment of a kingdom under the rule of God (Luke 10.9).

11

2.6    The Church of England's response to this is the ideal of a servant people in every community, with a leader who presides at their worship and encourages them forward in service and mission. Christians are required not only to care for each other but for anyone in need, regardless of station, creed or race. Clearly such an approach cannot be measured in terms of cost effectiveness nor can its results be objectively appraised.

2.7    The significance of the parish system is that it is the local, ancient and deeply rooted manifestation of the Church of England's nationwide service, worship and witness. The residents of every parish have the right to attend services, to receive the ministration of the Church and parish clergy, to be married in the parish church and (if space is available) to be buried within the parish. The parish system is an attempt to express the fundamentally personal and relational quality of the distinctively communal style of Christian existence. In Christian history it developed together with the office of the bishop, by which care was taken for the continuity and effectiveness of the Christian mission. Indeed the word *paroikia* (or 'district', the Greek word underlying *parochia* and parish) originally meant the ecclesiastical area under the bishop. From the later fourth century it came to refer to the subdivisions which the bishop put in charge of resident presbyters. Parish and diocese are thus essentially related, in a communion of mission shared by bishop, priest and people. The parish system is decentralised. Some of the central organisational structures have evolved in response to the need for the Church to deal collectively with particular aspects of its life and not because the Church of England is, by its nature, a centralised institution. The system also reflects, in the English context, the shared communion of bishop, priest and people.

2.8    The way in which this approach works in practice differs from place to place and from time to time. When there was little State provision in England and communities were smaller and more cohesive, the parish priest was a key figure in taking initiatives to alleviate suffering and provide facilities. He would visit and know his people, whether they came to church or not, and he would take the lead in establishing schools, hospitals and charities. To a greater or lesser extent he would be supported by the local worshipping Christians and some, such as churchwardens, were important figures in the whole community.

2.9    Today many of the works initiated by the Church of England have been taken over by the State. Other Churches and charities have taken important roles. Greater mobility and specialisation have meant that some provision is better made for a much wider area than the parish. The growth of cities has made it impossible for the priest to know the needs of more than a small proportion of his or her parishioners.

2.10    One response to these changes is to suggest the dismantling of the parish system. Particularly in suburban areas some parishes have attracted large congregations from a wide area and it is probable that significant numbers of worshippers in many parish churches no longer live within that parish's boundaries. Just as people travel to work or to reach other facilities, so some travel to other churches.

2.11    This development does not, we believe, detract from the fact that the parochial system provides the theologically significant building blocks of the Church of England's strategy for service. The gospel of redeeming love and sacrifice must take root in the immediate neighbourhood. A local church would not be true to its calling if it sent money and people across the world and neglected the needs of the people down the street. A Christian congregation should at least be attempting to create in the parish a community of mutual love and care even where social forces press in a more impersonal direction.

2.12    The Church must recognise the realities of how the parochial system can work today. It should not romanticise and have expectations more consonant with England of earlier centuries. The Church still rightly cherishes its ministry to every parishioner throughout the land, but in order to function in the twenty-first century the parish and the priest have to recognise that serving can only be adequately attempted in partnership with others. This requires the humility of recognising that other Churches and institutions are sometimes better placed to take the lead. It demands patience in developing local mechanisms whereby partnerships can be forged. In other words it means abandoning the worst features of parochialism while valuing the personal and the local.

2.13    Further, a priest has to recognise that there are now many people in the parish who are as well equipped as he or she is to offer various kinds of service. Others are capable of being trained to offer practical, pastoral and spiritual help as part of the mission of the whole people of God. This means that some of the traditional roles of the clergy are disappearing and the local priest needs to be trained to train, to build up and co-ordinate teams of ministries, to encourage, nurture and support the gifts of others, and to serve the unity of the whole Church. Much of this is already taking place and operating well but it demands a special kind of resourcing if service is to be developed as a main strand of the Church's mission strategy.

2.14   **Witness** is the third element of the Church's mission. We have chosen this word because it is clearly fundamental to the early Church's understanding of its task. The disciples were to be witnesses to Jesus and to his resurrection (Acts 1.8, 22). The first apostles derived their authority from the risen Lord and they were to exercise that authority by teaching what they had experienced and making new disciples. They witnessed the resurrection of the Lord and they witnessed to the Lord.

2.15   One of the most potent ways by which the early Christians witnessed was by a new form of corporate existence, embodying a distinctive personal lifestyle – a 'life worthy of God' as it was sometimes put. The evidence of the New Testament is frank about the frequent failures of both individuals and whole communities. But they succeeded sufficiently to attract others to the faith (as, for example, Acts 2.42-47 makes clear, a passage where the interrelatedness of worship, service and witness is very apparent).

2.16   Witness implied holiness of living, teaching the faith and evangelism, the third being the outcome of the first two. It is important to note for our purposes that from the first century care was taken with the continuity of the witness over time and with its unity and effectiveness across a locality, region or nation. Although early congregations developed their own styles against different social backgrounds, they were both supported and disciplined to ensure there was some consistency of teaching. Instructions were given to particular individuals to safeguard the authentic preaching of the gospel. There was concern about financial support for those who gave themselves to preaching. There were constant instructions to preserve unity in heart and mind and to avoid factiousness and division. But as the Church grew the problems became more complex, and a variety of levels developed corresponding to different specific conditions, boundaries, languages and cultures. A congregation (or a parish) which is isolated from authority and the support of others is threatened by idiosyncrasy and division. Moreover, each of those levels shares in the collective task of witness and makes its own distinctive contribution to the witness of the Church to the whole community at all levels.

2.17   We have briefly outlined the three tasks of the Church – worship, service and witness. They need to be clear in the totality of the Church's life in parish, diocese and nation. Providing proper care is taken with the continuity and effectiveness of the common witness to the gospel of Jesus Christ, each level will be able to trust the rest of the Church in the realisation of its mission. The local church should set clear objectives and make sound plans to meet them while being aware that effectiveness and efficiency cannot be measured only in managerial terms; by its nature the gospel of love is sometimes extravagant.

2.18    The parish must have freedom to make its own plans within the fellowship of the diocese and the national Church through which it finds much of its identity. The parish must be responsible for its own resources but also be prepared, in a spirit of trust, to give and receive from the rest of the Church as circumstances demand. It is to the question of resources that we now turn.

## The resources required to carry out the mission

2.19    The chief resource of the Church is the grace of God. No amount of structure and organisation can 'put the Church right' if, at every level, it is not turning to God for his provision. God the Holy Spirit is the creator, sustainer and life-giver of the Church. The Church looks to God for planning, strategy, resource and purpose. The means of God's grace come from Jesus Christ himself, the founder of the Church. The channels of his grace are scripture and sacrament as received and shared within the fellowship of the Church. The knowledge and use of these means of grace come to the Church within its established traditions and with the application of the graced reason of God-given minds.

2.20    The whole people of God look to him in these ways for their resourcing. At the heart of church life there is a continuing process of becoming aware of God and his purposes; of growth and change which makes the Church more like the body God wants it to be; of risk and exploration into the unknown. The basic resources which God offers are dynamic and presuppose a Church which is in pilgrimage and constant development. Each generation and each setting has to be ready for the surprises of God and to be open and flexible enough to respond to them creatively and thankfully.

2.21    That is why the present time in the life of the Church is such an opportunity. Now is the time (not the first and not the last) when we can review our resources and adjust the ways by which we assemble and share them in a clear and explicable way, yet leaving sufficient flexibility for responses to new invitations which God issues and for which he will continue to provide resources.

2.22    Within that context God in his grace has provided the Church with three main sets of resources – people, buildings and money. They

15

are interdependent and as a whole they are essential for the Church to carry out its tasks.

## The people of the Church, buildings and money

2.23   It is the people of any organisation who form the principal resource. Defining who the **people** are for the Church of England is complicated. There are some 13,000 parishes with approximately 10,000 parochial clergy, about 1.1 million regular church attenders and around 1.5 million people on church electoral rolls. Yet the Church of England also maintains a parochial system which offers 'a cure of souls' to all who live within the parish, regardless of faith commitment. Rights of baptism, marriage and burial still belong to the parishioner. Public opinion is difficult to quantify, but it seems that over half of the population still claim to be in one sense or another 'Church of England'. The structures which we set out in this report must be capable of serving all the people of this nation, worshipping or not, lay or ordained. The Church must have a sense of 'being' as well as of 'doing': its continued existence and presence in every community and its witness to the reconciling love of God are in themselves of great value, as well as the functions and acts of service which the people of the Church perform.

2.24   At baptism people are not only made members of the Church, with access to its teaching, sacraments and fellowship, but are also commissioned to witness to their faith by their lives. They are told to 'fight valiantly under the banner of Christ' and to 'shine as a light in the world'. How effectively they are able to do this will depend on the faith and confidence they gain within the life of the Church and the opportunities they take for service and witness in the world in which they live. Hence it is vital that resources are directed to teaching, guiding and supporting them.

2.25   Some of the people will take particular responsibility within the life of the Church. They will use their skills in administration, finance, leadership, care and teaching. A minority will serve the Church full-time in these capacities but most will give their time voluntarily in the setting of their local church. Care must be taken to nurture, encourage and co-ordinate their training and deployment, and resources need to be directed to this end.

2.26   Out of the whole body of believers the Church chooses ministers with particular authority and defined tasks. Many of these will be ordained to lead and service local congregations in their mission. There need to be nationally accepted and understood systems whereby such people are selected, trained, deployed and (in many cases) paid and housed. Ideally these systems will involve both the local church and the wider Church in order that their ministry is acceptable nationally and also has some kind of consistency.

2.27    The Church of England is fortunate to have the services of several hundred clergy and lay people who work as chaplains to the armed forces, hospitals, prisons, schools and universities or as diocesan advisers in many different spheres of life. It has Church Army evangelists, trained readers, and many who work in sector ministries, for example in industry, agriculture or among young people. The Church also has many other kinds of active voluntary societies such as the Mothers' Union. We affirm and endorse the valuable work they carry out in taking the message of the gospel to diverse, and often vulnerable, groups of people. Our report makes scant reference to them but this should not be taken to be a neglect of their contribution to the worship, service and witness of the Church. We believe that the structures which we recommend would enable the right decisions to be made about all the resources which God has made available to the Church.

2.28    In the Church of England every diocesan bishop is 'the chief pastor of all that are within his diocese, laity as well as clergy, and their father in God' (Canon C 18.1). It is the bishop's responsibility to seek out, train and authorise ordained ministers for every place within his diocese. The bishop has a special duty to uphold the authentic apostolic faith and to 'set forward and maintain quietness, love and peace' among all people. As we have described in chapter 1, this is a personal obligation, but at the same time it is shared collegially and communally. We discuss in our report the exercise of this role with a view to the coherent and effective leadership of the Church. The bishop must exercise his role in consultation with his clergy and the local congregations in his diocese, and with his fellow bishops and the lay and ordained people of the national Church. Such consultation can only be successful when all concerned are clear about objectives, have accurate information about resources and are in agreement about what decisions are made and by whom. Those who sustain the Church by their giving and voluntary service and those who have dedicated their lives to parish ministry have a right to expect some coherence in the way in which the resources they have provided are spent and the Church's ministry is deployed within their parishes. The proportion which lay people are now paying towards the cost of ministry is rising year by year and with this change has come an increased demand for greater accountability for the way in which the

Church's resources are used. The people of the Church who are supporting it with their giving are rightly seeking a Church which is both accountable and can demonstrate direction and vision.

2.29 The people need the resources of **buildings**. At the local level the essentials are a place for worship, housing for ministers and space for teaching and social occasions. In addition to parochial buildings the Church has cathedrals (the subject of a recent report by a separate Commission), houses for senior clergy including bishops, and buildings to house the administration of the Church in the dioceses and at the national level. At this point we wish simply to note that at present there is often confusion at the local level about who is responsible for which buildings and whether that responsibility carries any power for making long-term decisions about them. We believe buildings are an essential resource, in many cases a glorious inheritance, in others a great burden. The management of them deserves a more coherent structure which would enable the development of a long-term policy in which both national and local Church could participate, and in which the interests of the nation can be taken fully into account, rather than the piecemeal and largely reactive way of doing things which we have at the moment, and we mention this further in appendix C.

2.30 The resources of people and buildings themselves need to be resourced by **money**. It is important to see money as one of the many gifts of God and not simply as an unfortunate necessity. The theology of stewardship is not simply a way of getting people to give, but is essential to the Church's teaching about grace and generosity. Without a dynamic and positive attitude to money the Church will fail to provide enough to make proper use of this essential resource.

2.31 Almost all the Church's money is, or has been, given voluntarily. The Church charges fees for some of its services but these represent only a small percentage of its income. Its investments, locally, regionally and nationally, derive from assets which were originally given by pious benefactors. The financial objectives of the Church differ fundamentally from those of a commercial operation. It does not exist to make money or to pay cash dividends but freely to serve, and all its financial resources need to be seen against that wish to serve. Money is not a vulgar adjunct to the life of the Church. The Church must engage constructively with all aspects of the world in which it carries out its threefold mission. It must be vigorous in raising the money it needs and skilful and prudent in managing it.

2.32   Financial decisions are often best made closest to where the money is raised and spent. This breeds an atmosphere of trust and generosity. The more people in the local congregation understand exactly what the Church is doing and what resources it needs, the better they will respond. The vast majority of the Church's money is raised and spent by local congregations so it is important that efficient budgeting is set alongside policy making at that level.

2.33   But the Church's total operation means that some activities have to be carried out at regional and national level and we discuss the reasons for that later in our report. The financial machinery needs to be able to demonstrate clearly where these cost centres are and what are their purposes and requirements. The principal financial centre is the diocese which lies between congregations and the national level. The structures also need to involve the providers of money in the decisions about spending at regional and national level. As in any large and complex organisation, the problem may lie more in the communication of needs and resources than in the raising of money. This process of consultation, communication and decision-making needs to make full use of the synodical structures. One of the major tasks of our Commission is to remove the confusion which now surrounds the way in which the Church deals with its money. We must ensure that financial policy can be addressed and executed in such a way that the needs of the Church are given an order of priority and a clear indication of them is given to those who contribute to and manage the Church's money at all levels.

## Partnerships: common purposes and shared resources

2.34   The Church of England has obligations to, and benefits from, a number of partnerships. These help to sharpen its mission, as the established Church, to the nation and to broaden the context of its work. Our partners also offer opportunities for sharing resources so that common interests and objectives can be met more efficiently.

2.35   In terms of structures and resources we believe **ecumenical partnerships** represent a huge potential which is far from fully realised. The Council of Churches for Britain and Ireland and Churches Together in England are the national instruments for ecumenical action. This is reflected at regional level by county ecumenical bodies and many local churches belong to local ecumenical bodies.

2.36   Significant progress has been made in the sharing of vision, teaching, worship, buildings and ministry. In addition there are many informal meetings of church leaders and others. There are now around 750 local ecumenical partnerships through which resources are shared.

2.37   The structural links between the Church of England and other Churches are maintained through the General Synod's Council for Christian Unity and through the elected representatives on the national ecumenical bodies. However, each denominational Church remains independent within its own disciplines and structures and although important, the ecumenical dimension is not directly encompassed within the Commission's terms of reference. We note with enthusiasm that one of the Church's ultimate goals is full visible unity and for that reason are glad to regard our present concerns and proposals as provisional. We believe one of the crucial challenges facing all the Churches is how to turn structures of ecumenical co-operation into instruments for sharing responsibility and decision-making.

2.38   The Church of England, as an established Church, has a **formal partnership with the State**. While the basic question of establishment is, again, beyond our terms of reference, the fact of this special relationship does have important consequences for the Church's mission and structure. Both the Church Commissioners and the General Synod have separate obligations to Parliament, and the appointment of bishops and the role of the senior bishops in the House of Lords are other important aspects of the partnership between Church and State.

2.39   In terms of mission the established nature of the Church provides particular opportunities for service. We have noted that the parochial system (which in English history since the Reformation has been a feature of establishment but is not dependent on it) offers particular opportunities to, and makes certain demands of, the Church. The local priest and his parochial church council have obligations which affect the way in which they must manage their mission and their resources. For instance, a significant proportion of the parish priest's time is spent in pastoral work outside the immediate membership of his or her congregation. He or she visits the sick at home and in hospital, buries the dead, prepares for marriages and is available for counselling and care. The Church also plays a significant role in local civic life and maintains close relations with local authorities and the legal system.

2.40   At the diocesan level, cathedrals contribute significantly to the threefold mission of the Church and to its role in the life of the nation. Important parts of the Church's mission must also be carried out at national level. Worship, service and witness may still summarise all these aspects of the Church's work. If the national work of the Church is done well it can help create a setting, a climate of opinion, within which the parishes can carry out their mission and significant partnerships can be forged at the local and the national level.

2.41    There are also **partnerships with voluntary missionary agencies.** These include a large number of Anglican mission organisations working at home and overseas. They relate to the mission of the local church both by being an educational resource and by inviting partnership with the worldwide Church. At national level the Partnership for World Mission brings together the synodical and voluntary interests in this vital aspect of the work of the Church. It seeks to provide a means for the Church of England to relate to other parts of the Anglican Communion.

2.42    The voluntary agencies represent a considerable resource to the Church and we urge that the process of co-operation should be accelerated to remove unnecessary duplication. However, we recognise the vitality of the voluntary principle and believe that more would be lost than gained by an attempt to bring the major voluntary societies into one structure or under synodical control. The nature of grace and the untidy activity of the Holy Spirit will always produce initiatives which do not fit neatly into conventional structures.

2.43    The **partnership with the Anglican Communion** is of immense significance to the Church of England but does not fall within the scope of the work of this Commission. The Anglican Communion has its own secretariat based in London. The Church of England formally relates to the Communion whose focus is the Archbishop of Canterbury not only through the Archbishop himself and the machinery of the Anglican Consultative Council and Anglican Primates, but also through the General Synod Office and its various Boards and Councils. Provinces within the Communion are autonomous but the Communion gives them international and theological identity. The close links between the Anglican Churches in England, Ireland, Scotland and Wales are of particular importance given the extent to which they each relate to the same secular structures and national and cultural frameworks.

2.44    There is one important aspect of the Anglican Communion which relates directly to our concerns. By virtue of his historic office, the Archbishop of Canterbury is the unique focus of the Communion. This role puts great demands on him personally. He is responsible, for example, in consultation with the Primates of other provinces, for calling together the Lambeth Conference of bishops once every ten years.

2.45   At the same time the Church of England looks to the Archbishop of Canterbury as its national leader and he is often seen as the only person able to speak for the Church as a whole. This is a heavy responsibility but one for which he is given little executive power. The Archbishops of Canterbury and York both have complex, multi-dimensional roles and carry expectations which are all the harder to deliver because of the fragmented and incoherent character of the Church of England's own national machinery.

2.46   This brings us to the heart of our task. There are five perceived sources of executive authority at the diocesan and national level: the Archbishops; the House of Bishops; the diocesan bishop, the Bishop's Council, the diocesan synod and the diocesan office; the General Synod (and its Boards and Councils, including the Central Board of Finance); and the Church Commissioners. Although the burden of expectation tends to rest on the Archbishops, in fact all five share the objective of serving the mission of the Church at local and national levels, and would we believe broadly agree about the definition of the task as outlined in this chapter. But the way in which they relate to each other and interact with the rest of the Church has perhaps sometimes led to confusion at the very points where clarity of purpose is most needed. If the Church is to work as one body it must adopt a simpler approach to its tasks and a more trusting and flexible attitude towards institutional structures. A learning Church must grow used to change.

## The primary aims of the Commission

2.47   We see our task, therefore, as being to make proposals for structures and mechanisms within the Church, which will:

- communicate the purposes of the Church to the people of the Church and to the nation

- support, supply and affirm the local church in its mission of worship, service and witness

- manage effectively and efficiently the financial and legal framework in which the Church has to operate

- ensure that tasks are carried out at the most appropriate level

- witness, clearly and sensitively, to the nation

- sustain the Church under change.

2.48　We do not underestimate the complexities of this task, but we believe the Archbishops have chosen an opportune time for it, when the Church as a whole sees the need for change and has the will to think and plan in a radical way. Without that determination nothing which we propose will be implemented. We ask that this report will be received in the spirit of the prayer with which this chapter began, so that it may be answered.

# 3

# Why we must work as one body

## The shortcomings of the central structures

3.1    In the previous chapter (and specifically at paragraph 2.46) we pointed out that while executive authority rests in several places at the national and diocesan level, the way in which they relate to each other and interact with the rest of the Church has led to confusion. In this chapter we describe both the perceived and the real shortcomings of the organisations of the Church and give illustrations of the different kinds of difficulty which can arise.

3.2    Our concern is with the structures of the institutions, their cultures and the relationships between them. We focus on the lack of coherence *between* the different bodies. At present, the system impedes leadership. We believe there is a compelling need for reform, and that it is urgent. It is not our concern to allocate praise or blame for past events. Still less do we wish to criticise those who hold positions of leadership in the institutions of the Church or those who serve them. None of them has at his or her disposal the means to trigger the solution to the problems which beset the Church at the national level. They can only deal with the system as it is.

3.3    The constituent bodies of the Church of England form part of an inherently complex whole. They are the natural outcome of a long history of piecemeal development. Much of what goes on at the national level puzzles and dismays many in the parishes and the dioceses, who wonder how much confidence they can have in the central organisation of the Church.

3.4    It is easy to see why. The defects of the existing central structures of the Church might be summarised as follows:

● people are dissatisfied with and lack confidence in the national performance of the Church especially, in recent years, the Church Commissioners

● there is no single body with overall responsibility for co-ordinating those aspects of Church policy which are necessarily the subject of central planning, especially in relation to the allocation of resources

- there is a cat's cradle of autonomous or semi-autonomous bodies with distinctive, but sometimes overlapping, functions which are a source of confusion and wasteful duplication of effort

- much of the work of the national bodies is committee-bound

- there is no national equivalent to the coherence achieved in dioceses through the workings of the model of the Bishop-in-Synod.

3.5    The national institutions which are the subject of our review are the offices and roles of the Archbishops of Canterbury and York; the House of Bishops; the General Synod and its Boards and Councils and the Central Board of Finance; the Church Commissioners; and the Church of England Pensions Board. Each has its distinctive role and responsibilities but none can bring together all the policy and resource issues which the Church faces. This fragmentation means that there is no single focus of decision-making and strategic planning. The result is that people in positions of authority have no shared sense of collective responsibility for furthering the mission of the Church and for finding ways of addressing the problems. A great weight of expectation rests upon the Archbishops, but they have no adequate executive machinery through which they can meet such expectations.

3.6    There are some issues of policy and resources in which a large number of bodies at the national level are involved. While many people participating in the Church's governance can stop things happening, few (if any) can make things happen. Power is negative rather than positive. The system places a great burden upon (and potentially gives too much influence to) the few who try to co-ordinate its working and master its complexities. It absorbs energies rather than releasing them. The whole process of dealing with an issue takes more time and more effort than in comparable secular organisations. In the following paragraphs we give illustrations of the difficulties which arise.

*Pensions*

3.7    The most vivid current example of a serious problem which the Church might have foreseen long ago, if there had been a single body responsible for taking an overview, is the arrangements for clergy pensions. It has an impact at the national level, in the dioceses and in the parishes. Over the years the General Synod has decided, on the basis of advice from the Pensions Board and the Church Commissioners, in broad terms what level of support should be given to the retired clergy. The Church Commissioners have provided the funds and the Pensions Board has administered the scheme. The liabilities which now rest on the Church Commissioners for pension costs are very large indeed. When the Commissioners assumed responsibility for funding pensions on a non-contributory basis in 1954, expenditure on pensions absorbed 7% of their income. By the mid 1980s this had risen to 36% reflecting an increase in the number of pensioners, improved provision and the effect of stipend increases. By 1994 expenditure on pensions absorbed over 50% of the Commissioners' income, the losses incurred by the Commissioners (see paragraph 8.8) having accelerated the rise. On the basis of advice from the consulting actuaries Bacon & Woodrow, the Report of the Lambeth Group indicated (at page 22) that this could rise to 57% by the turn of the century, and to 90% by 2010 'rising thereafter if no steps were taken to change the present arrangement'. The Lambeth Group was critical that pension commitments on such a scale had been assumed without any detailed assessment of the long-term effect on the ability of the Commissioners to maintain their support of the Church in other areas.

3.8    The Diocesan Boards of Finance have been consulted in recent months about contributions to future service pensions. Neither the parishes, nor the dioceses and the chairmen of Diocesan Boards of Finance (DBFs) as such were directly involved in any of the past decisions about pensions. They have now been consulted by the Church Commissioners and the Pensions Board, neither of which is solely responsible for pensions policy, about proposals on which the final decision will be made by the General Synod. Although many different bodies are involved in discussions, it is not clear who should decide on a particular proposition to be put to the Synod. Many individuals are making valiant efforts to find a way through the problem but it is not possible to say that the overall responsibility for it lies with any one institution or at any one level.

*Diocesan and parish boundaries*

3.9    The current lack of any capacity for strategic initiatives at the national level can give rise to anomalies in the ways some matters are dealt with. One example is the way in which boundary changes are made. Changes to a deanery within a diocese or the creation of an archdeaconry are handled by the Church Commissioners under the Pastoral Measure, but the movement of a deanery from one diocese to another or the creation of a suffragan see are handled by the Dioceses Commission and the General Synod under the Dioceses Measure. Neither the Dioceses Commission nor the Church Commissioners has the power to initiate proposals so no strategic view can be taken at a national level on matters of diocesan or pastoral reorganisation, and change can only occur when proposals are put forward by a diocesan bishop.

*Human resources*

3.10   There are other areas where the practice of the Church leaves much to be desired but no single body is responsible for reform. The Church's management of its human resources – its most precious resource – is characterised by an incoherence in policy aggravated by confused structures. In relation to the ordained ministry, for example, there is no single plan for the optimum numbers needed and how they are to be trained and deployed, and for making the necessary financial projections and plans for how the costs of their stipends and pensions are to be met. Ideally, the Church should have a strategy which is mission-led rather than resource-led. It should look first at how many clergy it needs to meet its aspirations in serving the nation as a whole. It cannot, however, ignore the question of how to secure the resources to support them. The Church should also, for example, ensure that its discussions about the nature of the Church's current mission are taken into account when candidates are selected for ordination, so that their calibre and training for the ministry matches the demands of mission. Several different bodies are now involved and there is no link to ensure that decisions on numbers and personal qualities are always made alongside the decisions about the financial, training and development resources which can be made available, especially in the longer term. Central and diocesan bodies often strive to do their best, sometimes taking on responsibilities which are not within their core functions, but gaps remain. There is no strategic overview.

3.11   Policy in respect of ordination and of matters to do with the ordained and nationally authorised ministry of the Church rests with each bishop and is held corporately within the House of Bishops. The pattern in the diocese where the bishop is Father in God of the diocese, and the synod the representative body of clergy and laity meeting with the bishop, does not work in quite the same way at the national level. In dioceses, matters of ministry and finance can be held closely together in structures which deal with matters of deployment and pastoral issues as well as with finance. At the national level, the Advisory Board of Ministry (ABM) reports to the House of Bishops as well as to the General Synod, and also advises diocesan bishops in respect of individual candidates and many other matters to do with the ordained ministry. Many executive functions are delegated from the House of Bishops,

27

whilst ABM is answerable to the Central Board of Finance (CBF) and the General Synod over matters to do with the cost of training and its departmental budget.

3.12    The Advisory Board of Ministry is called upon to advise on national policy and strategy but those in turn depend to some extent on financial issues and policies which the Church Commissioners administer. The Commissioners deal primarily with the dioceses and are an executive body, whereas ABM is primarily advisory, and on matters of policy deals with the House of Bishops. The Commissioners also have responsibilities for some matters regulated by Measure. In many cases, such as pastoral reorganisation, those responsibilities consist of handling casework under the Measure and adjudicating in cases of dispute, but the Commissioners have no responsibility for developing the strategic policy underlying the Measure itself.

3.13    The House of Bishops does not have financial authority, yet its decisions about the ordained ministry can have financial consequences for others. Equally, financial pressures can dictate the dioceses' policy on ministry and so affect national recruitment, selection and training, irrespective of the policy of the diocesan bishop or the House of Bishops.

3.14    In dioceses, issues relating to training are usually dealt with together, including in-service training for the serving clergy, the initial and continuing training of readers, aspects of local non-stipendiary ministry training, training for specific lay ministries, and more general lay training and other non-statutory lay education work. It is important to train the clergy and laity together, but there are occasions when separate training is appropriate. The present structure of General Synod Boards distinguishes between training for ordained ministry, the responsibility for which rests with ABM, and for adult lay training (other than readers), which is dealt with by the Board of Education.

3.15    In the Church's management of its human resources there are times when conflicting pressures can arise from the House of Bishops, the General Synod, individual bishops and dioceses, the theological colleges and other bodies. Each is concerned to meet certain needs and so has developed its own attitude, interests and procedures which do not always mesh readily with each other. Expenditure on training for the ordained ministry and on contributions towards stipends and the payment of pensions constitute by far the greatest part of the spending of the Church at the national level, but it is not considered within a strategic framework or planned as a coherent whole.

*Policy issues*

3.16   Policy issues can also be difficult to resolve. The Church's views on matters of ethics or personal morality are of great importance, but there are occasions when demands for a swift public response to external events can show up, from another angle, the fragmented nature of the Church's central machinery. This is an area of teaching in which the House of Bishops has a responsibility, but there is some uncertainty about its role and it is difficult for it to maintain a dialogue with a large number of other central bodies. Those involved in handling a single issue can include the Archbishops, the House of Bishops, individual bishops, the General Synod's Board for Social Responsibility, and the General Synod's Communications Unit. The House of Bishops from time to time takes a lead in issuing major statements. The House is, however, currently a deliberative body which has only a small secretariat and meets at intervals of several months, potentially leaving a substantial gap in handling urgent topical issues day-to-day or week-to-week. There are usually a number of interested individuals and bodies but none of them can be said to be ultimately responsible for taking the lead in developing responses and initiatives at any one time. On matters of policy in general, there is no focus of authority for ensuring that the work done by various bodies is co-ordinated and much time, effort and persuasive power is expended (particularly by the Secretary-General of the General Synod) in trying to secure coherence.

*Financial resources*

3.17   It is clear from the evidence the Commission has received from the dioceses and the parishes that many of their concerns focus on money – at least as much on the way in which financial matters are dealt with at the national level as on the actual sums involved. Many have lost confidence in the national structures. They feel that the money which goes out of the parish may not be spent wisely or well, and at diocesan level the concern is that the dioceses do not know how much more they will be asked to contribute to the national level, or how often. The Commission believes the complexity of the present central organisation of the Church contributes to the confusion which surrounds the way in which the Church's finances work.

3.18   In fact the Church as a whole depends now, as it always has, on local giving. It is simplistic to blame the Church Commissioners alone for the current financial problems of the Church. The Commissioners were not established to settle the financial policy of the whole Church and it was never for them alone to take a grasp on the problems of the

Church. Indeed, it is arguable that the establishment and growth of the Church Commissioners (and their predecessor bodies) have to some extent been a diversion and served to disguise the challenges facing the Church.

3.19    From its early days the Church of England was supported locally by gifts, endowments and enforceable tithes, but there were always areas in which the support was inadequate. The Ecclesiastical Commissioners were established in the nineteenth century in effect to redistribute some of the wealth of the Church (and some funds which derived from the State) for the benefit of the poorer parishes. They provided relief in cases of sometimes desperate need. The Church Commissioners were never, as it were, the central funders of the Church. Their fund is closed and the income from it now largely committed, providing substantial contributions to the dioceses and parishes, mainly in the form of stipends and pensions for the clergy. Tithes have been abolished. The Church is back where it was, largely reliant upon local giving and endowments, though the problem remains that some parishes and dioceses are rich in historic endowments and current giving while others are poor. The important difference is that the Church now has synodical government: the structure is not one of taxation and authority but of giving and consent. The present generation of churchgoers is not endowing the Church as past generations did. It is in this context that the Church must face afresh the challenge of sharing resources between rich and poor. It cannot assume that that is the responsibility of one of the existing central institutions: it is the responsibility of the whole body of the Church.

3.20    The Commissioners have in the past used their own cash flow to ease the cash flow of the dioceses (e.g. through operating overdraft arrangements with non-penal rates of interest) and have stood behind the dioceses when serious problems have arisen. The continued provision of that kind of assistance from some source or other is one of the challenges the Church must meet. We believe God has given it the resources – both financial and managerial – to do so. We believe our recommendations could provide an effective instrument for tackling the inherent inequalities in the local endowments of the Church.

*The dioceses and the national level*

3.21    We find there is an inadequate expression at the national level of the relationship between the dioceses and the Church of England as a whole. The central structures of the Church, for example, do not themselves reflect the growth and development of administrative and financial structures within the dioceses. The links between the chairmen of

DBFs and diocesan secretaries, and those bodies at the national level which make decisions which have financial or administrative consequences with which they have to deal, are not particularly satisfactory. There needs to be much closer and more systematic communication and consultation between the administrative structures at the national and diocesan levels and more sharing of information and professional expertise. The dioceses participate fully in the legislative functions at the national level, but not in the executive function. It is still possible for the General Synod to legislate without first having precise information about the manpower and financial implications of its Measures for the centre and the dioceses.

3.22  The dioceses were asked by the Commission's Diocesan Perspectives Working Group in a questionnaire whether they felt diocesan boards tended to replicate work done at the national level. Several felt they did. The demarcation line seems reasonably clear if the centre's role is limited to matters which clearly need to be dealt with at the national level and the diocesan board seeks to interpret any national guidelines and policies in a way which is practical and appropriate to the local context. The expansion of diocesan administration, however, has often resulted in reports on the same subject being produced at the diocesan as well as the national level, at considerable cost in time and money. There is a perception in some quarters that some aspects of the Church's work do not directly touch on the work and mission of individual parishes and there is resentment at having to pay for such activities. This is an example of where a greater sharing of information and effort between the national level and dioceses, and between dioceses, would help to eliminate overlap or duplication.

3.23  Whilst dioceses have been able to make whatever changes they wish to non-statutory boards, they are severely restricted in what they can do as far as statutory boards are concerned. For example, the Diocesan Boards of Finance Measure 1925 sets out detailed provisions concerning the membership of the DBF. The duties of the Diocesan Pastoral Committee and of the Redundant Churches Uses Committee are both enshrined in the Pastoral Measure 1983. A considerable amount of legislation would need to be either replaced or simply repealed to enable deregulation on a wide scale to be effected. We urge that such a review should be undertaken. Until then, however, many difficulties could be removed by a systematic improvement in consultation and communication as well as by a wider acceptance of the need for the Church at all levels to work as one body if it is to make the best use of its resources.

*Communications*

3.24　It is crucially important that the Church has the means to communicate effectively what it is doing at all levels. Recent years have seen considerable steps forward at the national level, following the establishment of the Church House Communications Unit under the auspices of the General Synod. There is a more integrated presentation of Church developments to the media and within the Church itself. There is close and regular dialogue between the communications officers at Lambeth Palace, the Church Commissioners and Church House, and with the network of diocesan communications officers. Nevertheless, there is much further to go if the Church is to present itself to the nation as effectively as possible.

*Dispersed central administration*

3.25　The existence of so many different bodies leads, inevitably, to the cultivation of different practices and priorities. The evidence submitted to the Commission by the Statistics Liaison Group provided telling examples of the difficulties which can arise with setting priorities because of the institutional separation of the functions at the centre. The Group was set up in 1991 to ensure closer co-operation in this area between the national Church bodies, and to make available more widely the services of the Central Board of Finance's Statistics Department. It comprises an informal group of staff from the principal collectors and users of statistics in the national Church bodies, including the CBF, the Church Commissioners, the Pensions Board, ABM and the General Synod's Communications Department. In its discussions a number of issues have emerged which have a bearing on the Commission's work. The setting of priorities is one example. Although a wide range of statistics is routinely collected from the parishes, dioceses and elsewhere, there are a number of arguably quite important areas about which very little is known; and some statistics are collected which have a very limited use. The Church only has reasonably up-to-date information about the total costs of ministry because a one-off exercise in collating statistics from all the different sources was carried out in 1992 for the publication *Still Giving in Faith*, and the compilation of the approximate figures we set out in paragraph 11.11 of this report was far from straightforward. Every statistic collected and processed has a cost. Although we welcome the efforts of staff of different bodies to co-ordinate their work, there is no formal or authoritative mechanism by which relative priorities can be evaluated.

3.26   Terms such as 'stipendiary clergy', 'Sheffield men' and 'new churches' have different definitions according to which national body is using them. The distinctions are usually well understood within and among the primary users themselves, but are often lost on outsiders. Some form of standardisation of terms would be desirable, but given that each organisation uses these statistics in a precise way for particular purposes, such standardisation is unlikely to be achieved within the present structures.

3.27   There is a degree of overlap in the responsibilities of national bodies. A good example is in the field of clergy deployment. Dioceses are often not clear about who they should turn to for the information they need, and this can cause confusion. The Church Commissioners provide the base figures for the number of clergy, the CBF make further calculations and ABM is concerned primarily with overall principles and strategies. These distinctions are often not apparent to dioceses. This can also lead to difficulties in maintaining an agreed line on issues concerning deployment.

*Working cultures*

3.28   The separate bodies at the national level have inevitably developed different working cultures. They operate in different ways, which can be detrimental to the working of the Church. Problems can arise from excessive loyalty to one body. Communication between the various national organisations is limited. There is a risk of people not knowing what is happening or of duplicating each other's work. In general the Church makes great use of committees and standing bodies, often carefully balanced in terms of churchmanship, geographical representation, clergy and lay membership and so on, instead of assembling for a limited time teams with the skills needed to do a specific job. An issue which should be quite straightforward can be looked at repeatedly by different bodies with little value added. Little distinction is made between matters which need to be handled thoughtfully, carefully and with wide consultation, and matters which can properly be dealt with more swiftly and decisively. There is also an emphasis on producing reports rather than securing practical outcomes. When reports are produced, there is little emphasis on their implementation and follow-up. This focus on activity rather than action is reflected in the way the staff of the national institutions are expected to service the committee culture and maintain its processes, rather than to use their skills to manage the work so that clear decisions are taken and implemented. Those looking for scapegoats must, however, recognise that the central institutions of the Church are led and staffed by skilled and committed people who have themselves had to struggle with the institutional limitations of the bodies they serve. They, as much as anyone, deserve better.

*Evidence of the problems*

3.29    The written evidence which we have received suggests that many people agree with our analysis of the nature of the problems facing the Church. It was said that the Church was too often reacting to financial difficulties rather than viewing circumstances and opportunities dynamically and proactively. The Church, we were told, should be managed with vision and there should be greater co-ordination in planning and strategy between the Church Commissioners, Lambeth Palace and Church House. There were several requests for the establishment of a unified body absorbing many of the Commissioners' functions and accountable to the General Synod. Parishes were said not to have a clear idea who was responsible for policy and resource direction in the Church of England. Several local authorities commented that their links with the Church of England were valued and strong but were made more difficult by the Church's organisational complexity.

3.30    The Commission has drawn on the experience of those in the parishes and the dioceses who are already working with energy and commitment to meet the challenges they now face. The dioceses, through whom the money for national Church responsibilities is collected, need to be closer to and more involved in what goes on at the centre and to have more confidence in it. The national institutions of the Church may be in London, but its national life is not based there; it is in the dioceses and the parishes. Communications within the Church need to be improved so that the parishes and the dioceses have a better understanding of what is done at the centre and how it is relevant to the local life of the Church.

## The levels at which things are done

3.31    At the heart of our proposals lies a determination to ensure that the institutions of the Church play their rightful ecclesiological roles. Institutions cannot be expected to operate well when they struggle with matters with which they were not designed to deal.

3.32    It is important that things are done at the right level, so that nothing is done by the national machinery of the Church which in ecclesiological terms should rightfully be done (or in organisational terms can more appropriately be done) at the diocesan or some other level. Our proposals for the central structures take the Bishop-in-Synod as their model and focus on the bishop with his diocese as the pivotal unit of the Church. The social doctrine of subsidiarity (rooted in catholic theology) holds that the higher body is subsidiary to the lower, and that decisions should be taken at the lowest effective level. In the Church of England it can be said to apply especially to the relations between the national bodies and the diocesan bodies.

3.33    Planning for the mission of the Church is the responsibility of the bishop and his Council and diocesan synod, with whom the bishop discusses the plans for ensuring that 'in every place within his diocese there shall be sufficient priests to minister the word and sacraments to the people that are therein' (Canon C 18 'Of Diocesan Bishops'). These include pastoral plans for the parishes, the total number of clergy, a strategy for the ministry of clergy and laity, and the necessary budgetary provision.

3.34    The bishop shares his cure of souls for all who live within his diocese with the clergy of the parishes. When instituting a priest to the cure of souls in a living the bishop refers to 'your cure and mine'. The parish church is the main focus of the spiritual lives of most Anglicans. Its energy and vitality, or its lassitude and ineffectiveness, impinge most closely upon the way people are nurtured in the faith. Certain minimum conditions are specified and certain limits to authority are set, but a very wide freedom is given to priest and to people, to witness to God's reconciling love for all.

## National responsibilities

3.35    The Church works most effectively as one body when things are done at the right level. The Church of England does not have and does not need an omnicompetent centre. There are, however, functions which can only be, and have to be, carried out by the Church as a whole rather than in the parishes and dioceses.

3.36    The core of shared doctrine and liturgy lies at the heart of the Church's identity. The Church needs an authorised set of liturgies, which in Anglican tradition are vehicles of doctrinal understanding. They are prepared by a national Liturgical Commission and submitted for approval by the General Synod in terms proposed by the House of Bishops.

3.37    Major decisions about the ordained ministry, such as the ordination of women, must also be taken nationally. Ordination to the ministry is a matter for individual bishops, but because accreditation is national there is also an inescapable role for the national level in scrutinising and validating programmes for those training under bishops' regulations at theological colleges which take candidates from many dioceses. Such matters could not be determined by individual dioceses.

3.38    The national level has an essential role in giving expression to the being of the Church which is more than the sum of its parts, and in reflecting to those parts their significance in relation to the whole. There is a demand for positive leadership of the Church at the national level, providing vision, inspiration and guidance, and pointing a way forward for the Church. What is said at the national level is received by many who do not otherwise hear the voice of the Church. The centre has a missionary role of witness in relation to national institutions, to the rest of the Church and to the nation as a whole. The central bodies of the Church of England relate to the Government, to the central bodies of the other Churches and to the worldwide Anglican Communion. The Archbishops, the House of Bishops and the General Synod all have a role in the national witness of the Church.

3.39    The role of the centre in finance is largely a default mechanism which comes into play when 'subsidiarity' fails. Over the centuries the Church grew on the basis of independent priests and bishops supported by local endowments, gifts and tithes. There arose a need to provide support for poor parochial clergy by channelling to them funds from Queen Anne's Bounty, and, through the Ecclesiastical Commissioners, from the richer parts of the Church. The centre assumed implicit responsibility for the maintenance of the ministry of the Church of England to the nation as a whole in the dioceses and parishes. The State was involved in that process. It is that which underpins the financial role of the centre. That will remain for as long as parishes and dioceses remain unequally endowed. The amount of money needed to administer the essential national functions themselves is relatively small. The role of the centre in the maintenance of the ministry is to help the dioceses to ensure that provision is made for the cure of souls throughout the country.

3.40    Given the devolved nature of the Church of England, the relative independence of the dioceses and parishes and the unequal distribution of their resources, the risks the Church faces are of fragmentation and having areas which are not properly served. The centre has only limited funds and powers of persuasion with which to prevent this happening. There is a need to be clear about where the responsibility lies and about the essential interdependence of the different levels in the Church.

There is at present no focus among the central structures of the Church which enables any one body to raise the question of whether it continues to be acceptable for the Church as a whole to tolerate the accidental inequalities in the wealth of dioceses and parishes. No one body is in a position to consult the dioceses about what is now to be done to redress that imbalance. The centre needs to encourage the Church as a whole to take hard decisions and see them implemented.

3.41    Some other functions which have to be performed at the national level stem from the nature of the Church of England as a national institution. Church property is governed by special rules. Similarly, most clergy are not subject to secular employment law but to a special body of law governing their position as office holders. If the system of Church government and administration is to operate fairly and retain confidence it needs some nationally determined uniform standards to regulate, for example, its own electoral system. The Church therefore operates within a framework of legislation. There are also issues about which Church and State consult. These include marriage, education and the provision of chaplaincies in hospitals, prisons and the armed forces, as well as major ethical issues such as abortion or euthanasia. Decisions as to which redundant churches to preserve and which to demolish have to be taken at the centre on national criteria, bearing in mind national financial arrangements.

## Leadership

3.42    The Church therefore inescapably has to have a central machine and the perspective which that offers gives rise to responsibilities beyond its immediate functions. The pooling of data and knowledge about all the dioceses provides additional information about the life of the Church as a whole which is not available within any one diocese. The centre can see – albeit imperfectly – the broad challenges which face the Church. The Church needs at the national level to be capable of analysing what is happening in the life of the Church, of listening to concerns, of consulting and of proposing ways forward, and of providing the leadership to pursue those ways. The spirit and the manner in which that is done are of crucial importance to the life of the Church, and the Church now has the opportunity to tackle the problems of structure and culture illustrated in this chapter. The changes we set out in the following chapters are radical, but we propose them with confidence and optimism because we are satisfied that they not only go with the grain of the Anglican tradition but strengthen it.

# 4

# The basis of the
# Commission's proposals

## Introduction

4.1    The Church of England does not need a large centralised bureaucracy. Within the Church authority is dispersed. The real need is to ensure that the Archbishops, the bishops, the General Synod and others at the centre are empowered and enabled to work well for the dioceses and parishes for the good of Church and nation. Our concern has been to ensure that in future the functions carried out at the national level are only those which should be done at that level on behalf of the Church as a whole and that they are done coherently, economically and well. It is clear from the evidence we received that that is also what parishes and dioceses want.

4.2    Everything that we propose for the centre is subject to this overriding need for the national level to operate in support of, and as a complement to, the dioceses and the parishes, and to be seen to be doing so.

4.3    In this chapter we outline our basic proposals. In the chapters which follow we describe them in more detail. Our task has been to examine the machinery required for effective policy-making rather than ourselves to make substantive policy decisions. Our recommendations would not and could not of themselves solve the many issues facing the Church. They would, we hope, enable some of those problems, and others which may arise in the future, to be resolved in so far as they can properly be addressed at the national level. We make no pretensions to deal directly with the wide range of issues properly handled by dioceses, deaneries and parishes.

4.4    The Church leadership at all levels, but especially at the national level, must rise to the serious challenges facing it. The Church needs to sort out its finances. It is moving sharply away from its reliance on its historic resources and must find new ways of maintaining its ministry to the nation. It must stop being preoccupied with its own institutions. In an age of great spiritual hunger, it must extend its mission. The Church has a collective duty to work as one body, to improve its own morale and to present itself as an open, inclusive, attractive Church. It must use to the full its privileged position in the life of the nation to teach the truth of the gospel and to reflect the joy of the life we are offered in Christ.

4.5     In chapter 1 we pointed out that to speak of the Church's 'direction' and 'effectiveness' is to imply a grasp upon the mission which God has given to the Church (paragraph 1.9). The Church now lacks a vehicle which allows it, collectively, to take such a grasp and to share responsibility for the formulation of objectives. None of the existing central institutions is so constituted or placed that it could effectively (or appropriately) overcome the serious organisational problems we described in chapter 3.

## The Commission's core proposals

4.6     The Commission believes that the Church should have a new National Council to provide a focus for leadership and executive responsibility. The Archbishop of Canterbury would be chairman of it and the Archbishop of York its vice-chairman. Most of the existing central bodies would disappear or be overseen by the National Council.

4.7     Our proposals build on the distinctive Anglican ecclesiology of the Bishop-in-Synod. They are intended to clarify and sharpen the roles of the Archbishops, the House of Bishops and the General Synod. The purpose of the Council would be to enhance the operation of episcopal leadership and synodical governance and to restore confidence in the national institutions. The Council would provide a forum in which those who lead the institutions of the Church could act as an executive serving the Church. It would provide the consistent, coherent driving force the Church needs if it is to work as one body. The staffs of the Central Board of Finance (including the General Synod Office and the Synod's Boards and Councils), the Archbishops, the Church Commissioners and the Church of England Pensions Board would merge to form a single staff service under the Council. The Church Commissioners would be restructured but remain as managers and trustees of the central historic assets of the Church. Almost all their other functions, including decisions about the allocation of their income, would be transferred to the Council.

4.8     The Council would give the Church a stronger sense of corporate responsibility for its mission and well-being, for establishing its needs and priorities and for determining its overall direction. That unambiguous sense of responsibility is more readily established in the dioceses, but there is at present no focus for it at the national level. The Council should consciously focus on winning the co-operation of the dioceses and the confidence of the clergy and the laity in the parishes.

4.9     A National Council would provide the Church with a body at the national level capable of strategic thinking and planning. It would replace a number of the existing bodies which carry different responsibilities within the central structures of the Church – including the Central Board of Finance – and the Council itself should in practice find scope for further rationalisation. Its proposed composition, functions and tasks are described in more detail in chapter 5. The Council's relationships with the House of Bishops, the General Synod, the Church Commissioners and the Pensions Board and the consequences for them of the creation of the Council are discussed further in later chapters. Such a Council would result in clearer and more purposeful roles for the House of Bishops and the General Synod. It would provide support for the leadership of the Archbishops. It would help the whole Church to develop a vision of its broad direction for the future and strategies for delivering it. The Council would review the problems and challenges facing the Church and propose an ordering of priorities, seeking guidance from the House of Bishops and the General Synod.

4.10     Above all, at the present time, the Church needs an overview of its financial needs and resources in the parishes, the dioceses and the centre, and machinery to ensure that such resources as are now available at the national level are used strategically and to greatest effect. The Council would bring together the spending responsibilities of the General Synod and the Church Commissioners and ensure that the dioceses were consulted about decisions which affected them. It would build a single budget for all the central functions and ensure that the way the Church manages its money is transparent, efficient and well understood at all levels.

4.11     The House of Bishops would exercise its leadership by developing, with the assistance of the Council, a vision for the broad direction of the Church, offering it for debate in the General Synod and the Church as a whole. This vision would in turn influence the work of the Council, which would seek the guidance of the House of Bishops on its overall plan and strategy and then present them to the General Synod for endorsement. Building on the model of the Bishop-in-Synod, this would allow the bishops collectively to offer leadership to the Church, while also taking counsel and seeking consent. The House of Bishops would elect two of its members to the Council, which would also include the Archbishops and other bishops who might be chosen to chair key Council committees.

4.12 The Council would seek the endorsement of the General Synod for its outline strategy, presenting it for debate. It would prepare the budget for national Church responsibilities and present it to the Synod for approval, setting it within the wider context of an overview of the Church's finances as a whole. It would ensure that matters were properly prepared for debate, provide information and policy advice on all aspects of the work of the central institutions, formulate and promote legislation, and answer questions about its work. The leaders of the Houses of Clergy and Laity would be members of the Council and the Synod would approve the nominations of the other members of the Council. The Council would look to the dioceses to use the General Synod as an effective means of representing their views and concerns.

4.13 We believe that those who deal with diocesan finance should be more closely involved with the financial issues facing the Church as a whole and contribute to the strategic thinking of the Council. We therefore recommend that the Council should establish a Finance Committee which would include some of the chairmen of Diocesan Boards of Finance (DBFs). The Church is becoming increasingly reliant on voluntary giving in the parishes and dioceses and the DBF chairmen's knowledge and understanding of local Church finance should be brought to bear on the Council's work. This will be particularly important if, as we hope, the Council is to pursue vigorously initiatives to find fresh sources of funds. We believe that planning and organisation in the Church would be strengthened by this link between the central and other financial structures. The Council should foster a non-centralist climate in the administration of the Church, reflecting the changed balance of funding between the national level and the dioceses.

4.14 The Church Commissioners would retain their investment and asset management functions, but one of the Commission's key proposals is that decisions about spending the income which the Commissioners make available for distribution should pass to the Council, together with the related legal commitments, discretions and responsibilities of the Commissioners. The Council would become responsible for consulting dioceses and advising them on the forms and levels of the pay of clergy and licensed lay workers.

## Style and procedures

4.15 In future the dioceses would deal with a simpler structure at the national level, and it is of very great importance that the centre should establish effective communications with the dioceses, so that there is a free and regular flow of information in both directions and consultation on issues of significance. We hope the Council would be active in disseminating information about best practice among the dioceses and would make good use of information technology and telecommunications.

4.16 There are a number of informal groups in the Church of England in which diocesan figures such as archdeacons or diocesan secretaries meet regionally. There are formal regional groupings of bishops. We propose that all these groupings should be standardised into six regions. It would be entirely a matter for the dioceses to decide whether to deal with some aspects of their work on a regional basis but we believe there is scope for economies to be achieved through pooling certain functions and areas of expertise. From the national perspective, there would be advantage in being able to seek collective views on financial and administrative matters from the regional groupings of dioceses. The regional groups could also play a role in helping the centre to disseminate good practice. At the same time there is a need to cut down to its essentials the number of bodies involved in work done at the national level.

4.17 Issues of policy, human resources, buildings and money must in future all be dealt with together so that the implications for the Church at all levels are fully explored and debated. The Church needs the capacity for medium- and long-term planning, in consultation with the dioceses, to meet the needs of the Church and to secure the maintenance of its ministry. We believe our proposals would enable the Church to achieve these changes. We also believe the Church should plan periodic reviews of its institutions. It must be a learning community (see paragraph 1.8). Such reviews would allow the Church systematically to evaluate the appropriateness of its organisational structures so that it could plan to respond effectively to any change in circumstances, before they reach crisis point. We believe our proposals are appropriate in the present circumstances, but the structures which are implemented following our report should have an inbuilt capacity for change.

4.18 We propose that a single unified staff should carry out the executive functions of all the national bodies and provide the support for them. We want to see that staff developing a coherence and singleness of purpose which the present structures do not permit. Under the leadership of the Council the staff should work within a single framework, taking personal responsibility for carrying out the work directed by the Council.

4.19 The Church now tends to look to its employees to maintain services and processes rather than to advise and take initiatives. It under-values the skill of its staff. We must change that approach if we are to achieve a leaner and more flexible central machine. The Church must seek out the gifts and competences of all its people, including those who have intellectual, managerial and financial skills. Under clear leadership, staff must be given freedom to manage and more responsibility and accountability for directing the outcome of their work. The General Synod, the House of Bishops and the Council itself should concentrate on key issues and then give their staff the authority to get on with the implementation of their decisions, holding them to account for the way in which they do so.

## A time for swift action

4.20    Most of the changes outlined in this chapter are essential to an integrated package of reform: they should not be considered separately and we do not believe they could be implemented piecemeal. We believe they are urgent, and that uncertainty will damage staff morale. The gospels and the epistles of St Paul call on us to work as one body. Some issues by their nature have to be resolved nationally. We cannot all serve on national bodies but we all need to be able to relate to those activities, to expect those executing them to be accountable, yet ultimately to be ready to trust those who use their gifts faithfully in the furtherance of the gospel.

4.21    We believe that the Church of England underestimates its own strength and potential. Indeed, because so much of the most important work of the Church takes place in the parishes, deaneries and dioceses, it would be wrong to exaggerate the impact of changes at the national level. Within these limits, however, there is now a significant opportunity to improve the way in which the Church can work as one body. Our report seeks to build on the existing strong foundations of the Church, so that its potential can be fully realised.

4.22    Our proposals should not be seen as one in a series of options; they form an inter-related set of changes which should be considered as a whole. We include in appendix B a draft Measure to illustrate the kind of changes that might be needed to implement our recommendations. The detailed plans for implementation should be made in a spirit of co-operation and optimism. We hope our proposals will be debated widely and constructively. Our belief is that the changes of style and substance which we recommend must be implemented swiftly. If that view is widely shared, the Church must be willing to support its leadership and seek the strength of the Holy Spirit to sustain the will to make it happen.

# 5

# A Council for the Church of England

## The National Council

5.1　We have identified among the national organisations of the Church a lack of coherence which frustrates leadership and collective action. The proposed **National Council of the Church of England** whose composition and role we describe in this chapter would for the first time provide a single focus of leadership and executive responsibility within the Church.

5.2　The object of the Council is to enhance the operation of episcopal leadership and synodical governance within the Church, not to supplant them. We see a confident central organisation working with dioceses and parishes and in support of them, as a necessary aid to the effective overall mission of the Church. The Council would provide the springboard for a new partnership of mutual recognition and responsibility between dioceses, parishes and the Church at the national level.

5.3　The organisational changes we propose would require legislation to be passed by the General Synod. The Council would report to the Church through the General Synod, and in respect of the budget for national Church responsibilities it must be clearly accountable to the General Synod. It would not, however, be subordinate to it. That would be to confuse the roles of executive and legislature within the Church's governance. There needs to be a proper balance between Council and Synod, which is discussed at more length in chapter 6. The General Synod simply cannot be an effective executive body. The Council would not be an alternative to the Synod or to the House of Bishops, each of which exhibits the quality of representativeness in different ways. The Council's membership would combine elements of representativeness and of expertise in undertaking the tasks given it, but the emphasis should be on the latter because it would need to earn the authority of competence. The Council would exist to do a job of work and its credibility would come from its effectiveness in doing it. The Council should be large enough to reflect these various considerations but small enough to retain its own corporate coherence. Its members would have a personal and public responsibility for achieving results.

5.4     The Council would be the leading body within the national administration of the Church. Independent trustees would have discrete functions in relation to the assets of the Church Commissioners and pension funds. Whilst various executive bodies would continue to serve the Church at national level, they would interrelate through the Council. There is a need for a single framework within which the responsibilities and interests would function. Coherence and direction would be provided through the fact that:

- they would function under the guidance of the Council, part of whose task would be to ensure a shared perception among them of the Church's needs

- they would all be answerable in varying degrees to the General Synod

- they would have interlocking memberships

- they would be served by a common staff, employed by the Council

- they would occupy shared office accommodation.

In the following chapters of our report, we describe the Council and the interrelationships between the various bodies which make up the national organisation of the Church.

## Functions and tasks

5.5     The **functions** of the National Council would include:

- helping the Church to develop a clearer sense of direction, of the opportunities presented to it and of its needs and priorities if it is better to fulfil its mission in the world, drawing on the guidance of the House of Bishops, and offering the result for the approval of the General Synod

- ensuring that policies and strategies are developed to meet those needs and priorities, and to exploit opportunities accordingly

- overseeing the direction of staff and other resources at the national level in support of the agreed policies

- supporting the dioceses and helping them in their work, including co-ordinating their activities where they agree this is desirable in order to help them better to achieve the Church's overall mission.

5.6     The specific **tasks** of the Council would include:

- assessment of the overall financial and human resource needs of the Church, and planning ahead accordingly, including not only the effective stewardship of these resources but taking active steps to enhance them

- determination, within a framework agreed by the House of Bishops and the General Synod and after discussion with the dioceses, of the allocation of income from the Church Commissioners' assets

- management, in discussion with the dioceses, of arrangements for redistributing resources within the Church to help even up the financial position of dioceses and respond to the needs of mission, and for the proposed apportionment of national costs among the dioceses

- submission for approval by the General Synod of the budgets for training for the ministry and national Church responsibilities

- presentation to the General Synod or the House of Bishops, as appropriate, of legislative or other proposals designed to help the Church respond to its needs and priorities, and to enhance the effectiveness of the Church's ministry and mission

- overseeing as necessary the work of the committees or Boards of the Council (see below) and of its staff.

5.7    In carrying out these tasks, the Council and its subordinate bodies would, under the terms of legislation approved by the General Synod, assume the present roles and functions of the Standing Committee of the General Synod and its Policy Committee, the Central Board of Finance of the Church of England and the Advisory Board of Ministry, all of which would cease to exist. The work of the other Boards and Councils of the General Synod would come under the authority of the Council. The constitutions of the Boards and Councils create rigid structures and the Council would need to be free to arrange the work for which it was responsible with more flexibility. The Council would assume most of the role and functions of the Church Commissioners for England (other than their trustee responsibilities and asset management role – see chapter 8). The experience of the last few years in particular has, we believe, amply demonstrated the need for the functions at present dispersed among these bodies to be brought together if issues facing the Church are to be tackled effectively. Providing, as we shall propose, effective accountability is built into them, the new arrangements should produce simpler, clearer and less cumbersome structures with more scope for purposeful and coherent leadership.

# The membership of the Council

5.8    If the Council is to provide the effective focus of leadership and vision we believe to be necessary, it would need to include among its members those who carry leadership responsibility within the Church at national level. Principal among these are the Archbishops of Canterbury and York. Other key clergy and lay figures would also need to be included.

5.9    The Council would not be simply a gathering of the Church's 'great and good'. Its members would need to share a corporate sense of responsibility for the mission and well-being of the Church. They should include those who carry key executive responsibilities within the Church's national life. The Council would not be a talking-shop but would be charged with fulfilling real tasks of crucial importance in the life of the Church. Its members would not be representatives or delegates but a group of key figures ensuring that the institutions of the Church work as a coherent whole.

5.10    The Archbishop of Canterbury as chairman and the Archbishop of York as vice-chairman would lead the Council. They would be immediately supported by four people responsible for the main areas of activity of the Council:

- a resources for ministry (human resources) chairman

- a mission resources chairman

- a heritage and legal services chairman

- a finance chairman.

5.11    These four part-time executive chairmen would exercise responsibility for leadership in each of these areas. They would work closely with the Archbishops in the development of the Church's overall strategy. Each of the four chairmen would be expected to assume a public leadership role within the area for which they were responsible. It would be their task to ensure the effective development of the Church's policies and the optimum deployment of its resources. Assisted by their staff, the chairmen would be expected to lead, to support and advise the dioceses, and to represent their own areas of responsibility, within the Church and outside it. They would also share in a collective responsibility to the Church as members of the Council. These would be demanding roles, calling for imaginative, management and presentational skills of a high order and a considerable commitment of time. They would, in this sense, mirror the sort of qualities required at present in the First Church

Estates Commissioner or the chairmen of, for example, the Advisory Board of Ministry or of the Central Board of Finance.

5.12    The four executive chairmen would be nominated by the Archbishops and their appointments would be approved by the General Synod. In view of the crucial significance of these appointments when the Council first came into being, the Archbishops would make their nominations on this first occasion after discussion in a special **Nominations Committee**. The members of that Committee, in addition to the Archbishops, would be the Prolocutors, the chairman and vice-chairman of the House of Laity, the First Church Estates Commissioner, the retiring chairman of the CBF, the chairman of the present Appointments Sub-Committee, the Archbishops' Appointments Secretary and the Secretary General. Although it seems likely that the finance chairman would be lay and the ministry chairman a bishop, there would be no prior requirement other than that these important posts should be filled by the person (lay or ordained, male or female) best qualified for the job. Appointments to these positions would normally be for between three and five years, renewable for one further such period. In making the initial appointments care should be taken to stagger the period of service so that all do not come up for renewal at the same time.

5.13    The clergy and lay leaders in the General Synod (the Prolocutors of the Convocations of Canterbury and York and the chairman and vice-chairman of the House of Laity) would also be members of the Council. The remaining members would be:

- two members of the House of Bishops (elected by that House)

- the Chairman of the Business Committee, who would be elected by the Synod from among the members of its Houses of Clergy and Laity. Again the guiding principle should be the election of the best person for the job

- the Council's chief executive and head of staff, the Secretary General (see paragraph 5.42).

5.14    We believe that the Archbishops should have an additional power to nominate to the Council people of quality who would bring to it skills and experience, essential to the fulfilment of its task at any particular time, which might otherwise not be available to the Council and would add to its strength. The General Synod would approve such nominations. For example, it might be appropriate to appoint a DBF chairman and/or some younger people among this number. This power should be permissive and limited in that there should not at any time be more than three such people on the Council (in addition to any of the executive chairmen who are found from outside the members of the General Synod).

5.15 This would give a Council of up to 17 members. All the members of the Council not otherwise members of the General Synod (that is such of the four executive chairmen as were not already Synod members plus any other appointees (see paragraph 5.14) and the Secretary General) would be *ex officio* members of Synod so that they could present the Council's business to Synod and be answerable to it. Any member of the Council would be eligible to be appointed to the posts of executive chairman described in paragraph 5.11.

5.16 By bringing together functions at present spread throughout the national level of the Church, the Council would identify clearly where responsibility lay for tackling pressing issues. It would be responsible for planning ahead and getting things done, and would have the capacity, commitment and 'clout' to do so. The Archbishops, the House of Bishops, the Synod and the dioceses would have an instrument for helping them articulate their vision for the Church and a means to give it strategic effect. There are three pressing practical examples of how it could help:

- for the first time, all the responsibilities at national level for ministry would be brought together in one place so that a coherent strategy for ministry and training for ministry could be developed

- for the first time, a single body at national level would be responsible for overseeing the financial flows within the Church, and for helping the dioceses and parishes in managing them

- for the first time, a single body would be responsible for developing with the dioceses a comprehensive pensions policy and arrangements for financing that policy.

## The supporting structure

5.17 To help it fulfil its role of developing and implementing a strategy for realising the vision for the Church which is articulated by the House of Bishops and approved by the General Synod, the Council would need a supporting management and committee structure. It should in our view be for the Council itself to decide exactly how this should be established and function. It is important to the new approach we wish to see the Church adopt that there should be expertise and flexibility in the way it handles its business. Coherent with the overall vision of the Church's mission, the Council should be free to build and amend its own supporting structures. It might, for example, wish to adapt some areas of its work to meet the developing requirements of the dioceses. It might wish to adjust some arrangements, for example in line with changes made by ecumenical partners. In some fields its work might grow or shrink from time to time. We recommend that the Council should keep its supporting structures under constant review to ensure that they provide no more than is absolutely necessary to ensure that the work of the Council is carried out effectively. It may well be that, especially in the initial period of implementation of this report, the Council would find it helpful to engage outside experts to advise on the process of changing the structures and the working culture at the centre.

5.18   The Council must not become self-contained and should work always in close relationship with the House of Bishops, the General Synod and the dioceses. In principle, as the diocese is the fundamental unit of the Church, the centre should be kept to a minimum. If there is any doubt about the need for a role or function at the national level, the bias should be against taking on that role or function.

5.19   Appendix C contains the outline of a possible model for this structure. We believe it would be a sensible starting point for further thought, but the Council must be free to organise things as it sees best. In chapter 1 (paragraph 1.8) we emphasised the need for the Church to be a learning community. Its structures should be capable of being adapted in the light of experience or changed in response to changing circumstances. The principal features of the structures suggested in appendix C are:

- **a resources for ministry department** – which would bring together responsibility for different aspects of ministry presently located in the Advisory Board of Ministry (which it would replace), the Church Commissioners, various Archbishops' Officers (principally the Clergy Appointments Adviser), the Church of England Pensions Board, and the Board of Education's adult education work

- **a mission resources department** – which would be concerned with sustaining the mission of the Church in its widest sense and with the effective use and co-ordination of the resources for mission of the Church at national level, including the work of the present Board of Mission, Council for Christian Unity, Board of Education and Board for Social Responsibility

- **a heritage and legal services department** – to encourage the best use of its buildings in furthering the Church's mission and to help the Church discharge effectively its responsibilities towards the national heritage; and to discharge responsibilities for legal and related services to the Council and its supporting departments, the Church Commissioners, the General Synod, the Pensions Board and the Church's tribunals and courts at provincial level

- **a finance department** – to direct, under the oversight of the Council, the national financial policies of the Church.

A central secretariat would service the Council and the House of Bishops, and the Council would be responsible for securing effective communications both within and outside the Church. The Council should have independent external auditors and an Audit Committee (with an independent element in its membership) to strengthen the processes of accountability.

5.20   More important than the actual structures are the principles and approach which we believe the Council should have in mind in addressing these matters:

- the supporting organisation should be as simple and light as possible, but must have adequate expertise in each area of work

- it should bring related pieces of work together and identify clearly where responsibility lies

- it must be clear how that responsibility is to be discharged and accountability met

- within a framework of accountability, people must be trusted to get on with the job and be given the means to do so

- there should be less emphasis on on-going committees and more on using the skills of staff and groups of people in relation to a particular task. The roles of the executive chairmen and their supporting directors would be crucial to the achievement of this.

5.21   It is essential that in viewing the role of the Council and its supporting organisation, the temptation to focus on committees and re-invent the plethora of them which abounds at present should be resisted. Of course, committees will be the sensible way to work in some instances. But they are not the only way nor always the right one. Our organisational proposals envisage a balance in each area between a part-time executive chairman, a director and supporting staff, and a committee structure kept to the essential minimum, all operating under the authority of the Council which would carry ultimate responsibility and decide its own organisational support. Initially most of the Boards and Councils of the General Synod would remain, but they would come under the Council and we envisage that the Council would quickly review their work and seek to cut down substantially the number of committees involved.

## How the Council would work

5.22    The new Council would, we believe, tackle directly and with energy issues which because of the present fragmented organisation are now addressed only with difficulty, if at all. It would be clearer where responsibility lay, and who was in a position to take action. With greater clarity would come greater visibility and transparency, and improved communication and information flows. In this way some of the basic requirements for effective accountability would be met.

5.23    The new organisation should also engender a greater personal and corporate commitment to making things happen. The many people who serve on Church bodies at the national level undoubtedly feel committed to what they do, but often they do not carry any personal responsibility for delivering in practice the ends which they have willed. Moreover, there can in some instances be too ready an assumption that the purpose of someone's membership of an organisation is to guard a particular interest (for example, of the laity or of the clergy, or of a particular type of church-manship) rather than to work positively for the advancement of a shared purpose of the Church. With its emphasis on people sharing in a common task and taking personal responsibility for its delivery, the new organisa-tion should provide an opportunity to transform the negative power which characterises many of the Church's present bodies into a positive one.

5.24    We envisage the National Council meeting some six or seven times a year (i.e. about the same number of times as the Standing and Policy Committees of the General Synod combined do at present). The Council should provide one of the major means by which the Archbishops can seek to exercise their personal responsibility of leader-ship in the Church. The Council would be required to focus on major issues of policy and to think strategically. On these matters it would be informed by the thinking undertaken by its executive chairmen and directors, in its major committees, and by its staff.

5.25    At present there is a tendency in the Church to think that the answer to every problem is to throw a committee at it and to assume that the committee must be carefully balanced between episcopal, other ordained and lay members, men and women, the Provinces of Canterbury and York, and so on. Once such a committee is established it can easily assume a life of its own. The new organisation should be slimmer than its predecessors and involve fewer committees and fewer members on each. There should generally be fewer layers through which work would have to progress, especially once the Synod's Board and Council structure has been reviewed, and less of a need than at present to take proposals through a variety of laborious procedures and different interested bodies.

5.26    In future, we believe that the purpose and achievement of every committee or group should be subject to regular review. As few standing bodies should be appointed as possible. More work should be done in small groups including experts or in *ad hoc* task forces with a specific focus and a limited life. As much as possible should be left to staff to execute within policy guidelines set by the Council and its committees.

## Powers, relationships and accountability

5.27    The new Council would be established by Measure. Legislation would be required to transfer certain responsibilities and powers of existing bodies, such as the Church Commissioners and the Central Board of Finance, to the Council. The Council would also be a body corporate, and so be able to hold property and employ staff. It would be a charity having as its object the furtherance of the work of the Church of England. Appendix B contains an illustrative draft of a Measure which would embody the main powers of the Council and the other changes we propose.

5.28    The Council's authority would derive from its effectiveness in undertaking the work entrusted to it. The likelihood is that its members would come from somewhat different backgrounds in theology and experience and its style of leadership would have to reflect the wisdom of Anglicanism in enabling the public expression within the Church of differing points of view. It would not and should not be a means of smothering dissent.

5.29    The Council would function within a network of accountabilities and checks and balances among various key bodies at the national level. In addition it would operate through a much clearer partnership with **dioceses** and through them with **parishes**. This would be achieved not only through the key role played in it by bishops and elected members of the General Synod but also through the proposed direct representation of Diocesan Boards of Finance (DBFs) on the Council's finance committee. In turn the DBF representatives would relate to a functioning regional network (see chapter 10). This would replace the present somewhat indirect representation of DBFs on the Central Board of Finance and should considerably strengthen the central machinery.

5.30    The Council would relate closely to the **General Synod** in respect of each of its main functions. Several of the Council's members would be elected by the Synod, and the rest would be appointed by the Synod on the nomination of the Archbishops. The members of the Council would sit in the General Synod and answer questions about their stewardship. The Council's direct contact with the dioceses and consultation with them should ensure that diocesan concerns are fully taken into account in the day-to-day work of the Council. While for the reasons set out in paragraphs 6.19 to 6.21 the Synod cannot itself act as an executive, the Council would seek the Synod's endorsement for the strategy it would develop and propose. The approval of the Synod would be required for any legislative proposals formulated by the Council, and for the budget for training and national Church responsibilities framed by it. The Council's relationship with the Synod is described further in chapter 6 (paragraphs 6.29 to 6.33).

5.31    Within the Synod, the leadership role of the **House of Bishops** is crucial. The Council would seek the guidance of the House of Bishops on the broad direction of the Church and the House's approval of the strategy which the Council developed in response before it was presented to the General Synod. The role of the Archbishops and of the two bishops elected by the House to be members of the Council (and of any other episcopal members of the Council) in planning the business of the House and in dialogue with the Council would be crucial. The Council would account to the House of Bishops for those aspects of the work of the national office of the Church (such as selection and training for the ordained ministry) which fell specifically within the House's responsibilities.

5.32    We have indicated earlier that we believe that the Council should take over responsibility for all the functions of the **Church Commissioners** other than that of managing the historic assets of the Church. We take this view because decisions about the detailed allocation of money generated by those assets should not be separated from a perception of the Church's priorities for mission. Nor should decisions about pastoral casework, for example, be divorced from a framework of policy on how the Church is going to deliver its ministry which the whole Church has discussed and owned.

5.33 Decisions about the management of the Church's historic assets would rest with the Commissioners, but the Council would be able to offer advice to the Commissioners on the needs and interests of the Church. The Commissioners would be expected to have regard to those interests, to any such advice, and to views expressed by Parliament and the General Synod. The final responsibility for the assets would, however, rest with the Commissioners. The proposed role of the Church Commissioners is described further in chapter 8.

5.34 We believe that the new arrangements we propose should strengthen **accountability** rather than weaken it. We see effective accountability lying neither in the perpetuation of large committees containing representatives of various interests, nor in the proliferation of formal checks and balances to the point at which action becomes impossible, but in giving people (whether Council members or staff) clear responsibility for doing a job, the means with which to do it, and holding them to account for the result. Our proposals seek to make accountability real rather than illusory.

# The Central Board of Finance

*Background: the Central Board of Finance*

5.35 **The Central Board of Finance** (CBF) is the financial executive of the General Synod and also has a formal role as the financial advisory body of the Church of England. It is proposed that the Council should take over its functions. The Board is responsible for the preparation and presentation to the Synod of an annual budget, for the management of all the Synod's funds, for advice on and co-ordination of the finances of the Church as a whole, and for collecting and tabulating parochial statistics of Church membership and finance. It is the employer for staff of the General Synod and its Boards and Councils. It has various other functions including the promotion of Christian stewardship, publishing and the provision of certain office services for the Synod.

5.36 The Central Board of Finance has a number of responsibilities which it exercises quite independently of the Synod. It administers the Central Church Fund, which receives legacies, subscriptions and donations and provides assistance to parishes and dioceses for special projects, towards training for ministry in the Church, and occasionally for urgent and unbudgeted needs at national level.

5.37 The Board is also responsible for the investment management of the Investment, Fixed Interest Securities and Deposit Funds established under the Church Funds Investment Measure 1958 for the trustees of charitable funds whose objects are connected with the work of the Church of England. There are nearly 50,000 accounts open in the three funds whose total assets amount to over £900 million. The investment office is operated by an associated company, Church Charity and Local Authority (CCLA) Investment Management Limited, which provides investment services to the Board and is authorised to give investment advice to Church bodies.

5.38 We recommend that the role of the CBF in overseeing and administering the Central Church Fund and in overseeing a number of other trust functions (including property interests) should pass to the Council. Similarly, the Council would assume the role which the CBF currently exercises as majority shareholder in CCLA. We envisage that these trusts would continue to be held separately but it is inherent in our proposals that there should be coherence at the centre. We therefore believe that the National Council should have ultimate responsibility for the allocation, within the terms of the respective trusts, of monies made available through the Central Church Fund for the general purposes of the Church of England, since the Council would be best able to discern where the funds are most required. In this way, all the functions vested in or exercised by the CBF would pass to the Council, which we envisage would delegate many of them to its Finance Committee, on which we propose the dioceses should be represented.

5.39 The Church Commissioners and the Council (as well as the pensions fund) will have substantial investment responsibilities including, in the case of the Council, the funds at present managed by the CBF Investment Office. It will be for each of these bodies to determine how best to discharge these responsibilities and whether, for example, to operate their own investment team or to engage outside professional management. Relative costs are an important consideration here and *prima facie* there must be a case for examining whether a single investment management team might be established. The CBF Investment Office, for example, which operates within a separate and self-financing company (CCLA Investment Management Limited) and which currently administers charitable and local authority as well as Church funds might be given the opportunity to bid competitively to manage some or all of the other funds.

5.40 In all the portfolios, ethical investment considerations will continue to be important and as a minimum we recommend that a small joint advisory group drawn from the Council, the Commissioners and the Pensions Board should advise on ethical investment matters. This would replace the Ethical Working Group which operates between the different existing bodies.

## The staff of the Council

5.41 The **staff** of the Church at national level are a very important resource. Highly skilled in many different ways and dedicated to the Church's service, they live day by day with the complexities and frustrations inherent in the Church's present fragmented national organisations. The new arrangements we propose would, we believe, enable their energy and skill to be deployed more creatively and productively. Within the new structure it would be clear to them and to others who was responsible for what, and to whom. The changes in the style of working which we see as an essential part of our proposals should free them to direct their energies to the achievement of ends rather than to maintaining elaborate committee structures and processes, which consume staff time and resources. Bringing all the staff of the national organisations (including those of the Archbishops, of the Church Commissioners and the Church of England Pensions Board as well as of the Central Board of Finance) under the Council as the single common employer should offer more opportunities to develop individual staff and to further their careers, as well as enabling a more flexible deployment of the Church's limited and tightly-stretched staff resource in meeting the changing pattern of demands on the Church. The employees of the Council would share common conditions of service which would need to be worked out in consultation with existing staff and their representative organisations. Although they may be serving different bodies, and would be unambiguously responsible for helping to discharge the duties of the particular part of the national organisations for which they work, their contracts should permit their flexible redeployment as the Church's needs or the interests of their own career development require.

5.42 The staff would be headed by a **Secretary General** who would be the chief executive officer of the Church at national level. It would be his or her job to lead all the staff of the Church at that level. The senior staff team would help provide the dynamic, strategic initiative the Council would need to fulfil its role. We have used the title Secretary General because it is one with which the Church is already familiar and because others (such as Director General) might carry misleading connotations. But the job would be wider than and different in nature from that of the Secretary-General of the General Synod, or any of the other senior staff posts in the Church at present. It would be a new appointment. The Secretary General would be appointed by the Archbishops of Canterbury and York after consultation with the Council and with the approval of the General Synod.

5.43　The Secretary General should be a full member of the Council, its committees and subordinate bodies. We believe that would be appropriate because of the responsibility which the Secretary General would share with the Council's other members for the executive leadership of the Church at national level. We are aware of the risk of focusing too much power in the hands of the Secretary General. It is, however, arguable that the lack of coherence and effective oversight in the present structures hold greater potential for the exercise of substantial influence. We believe that his or her undoubted influence would be tempered in practice by the Council's other members and by the Secretary General's answerability in Synod for matters within his or her remit. Moreover, there is a balance to be struck between on the one hand encouraging staff to manage effectively and, on the other, holding them to account for the result. With the Secretary General as with other staff, it is better to recognise their potential for influence and to make it properly accountable than to attempt to ignore it. We encourage the Church to welcome the gifts of all its staff at national level and to see them as wise, skilled and committed fellow servants, not as mere bureaucratic functionaries.

## The offices of the Council

5.44　We believe that the process of working together as one body, and transcending sectional loyalties and the cultures which can develop within different organisations, would be substantially enhanced if most of the new combined central staff worked together in one building. We commissioned chartered surveyors to report on how this could best be achieved and they identified three options. First, the new national office could be located in the Church Commissioners' premises at 1 Millbank. However, we were advised that major refurbishment or redevelopment would be needed before Millbank could provide enough space which was conveniently laid out and appropriate to accommodate the staff who now work in both Church House and the Church Commissioners. Second, the national office could be at a new location in a low cost area, perhaps near Lambeth Palace. Modest capital savings would be realised but only in the long term; and security and accessibility for staff and visitors would be less good. Under either of these options a debating chamber would have to be hired for meetings of the General Synod.

5.45    Third, Church House could become the site for the new national office of the Church of England. Church House is in good repair, having recently undergone a major refurbishment, and there would be sufficient space to accommodate the envisaged number of staff, based on an industry standard *per capita* square footage. Part of the income that would arise from reinvestment of the capital received from the sale of 1 Millbank would cover the extra occupancy in Church House. It would still be possible for conference centre facilities to be made available in Church House to outside bodies, an operation which has been successfully and profitably developed in recent years.

5.46    If all the national staff were in future to be located in 1 Millbank, we believe the ownership of that building should vest in the Council. Church House is owned by the Corporation of the Church House, an independent body founded by Royal Charter. If the national staff all worked in Church House, we recommend that the Charter should be amended so that the membership of the Corporation consists only of the membership from time to time of the National Council. The Corporation's officers would still be required to answer questions in the General Synod, which would also continue to appoint some representatives to the Corporation's governing Council.

5.47    We think it right that the National Council as the employer of all the staff of the national office should own or have effective control of the building in which they work, so that it can properly discharge its responsibilities in relation to working conditions, can control costs and can make strategic decisions about where staff are located. It would only be right for a more detailed study and a full financial appraisal of the options to be undertaken before a decision was taken. Nonetheless, our provisional view, based on the evidence we have seen, is that as far as possible all the Church's central staff (other than the Archbishops' personal staff) should be based at Church House, Westminster. In the longer term the Council should consider whether part of the Church's administrative staff should be relocated out of London. The priority, for the first few years of the Council's life, must however be to have all the central staff not only sharing a common employer but also, as far as possible, based in one building and we have been encouraged to learn that this could be achieved at Church House within a period of about five years, given certain assumptions which we believe to be reasonable. In the shorter term, the new Council and its senior staff will need to master the entire range of work carried out by staff in both the present buildings and to ensure that the important task of creating a single staff team with a new culture and unified purpose is not impeded by having to use two buildings rather than one.

# 6

# The General Synod

## Background: the General Synod

6.1   Synodical government in the Church of England came into operation in 1970. Before then there were two sets of national ecclesiastical bodies:

(a)   **The Convocations of Canterbury and York,** which are entirely clerical bodies dealing primarily with matters affecting doctrine and worship. In origin the Convocations are among the oldest legislative bodies in England having greater antiquity than Parliament itself. They had the right to make Canons, which were binding on the clergy. The Convocations could meet only if summoned by Royal Writ, and could only promulge Canons after receipt of the Royal Assent and Licence. Although they no longer have the power to make Canons, the Convocations still maintain a separate existence and meet occasionally. Each Convocation consists of an Upper House of Bishops and a Lower House of Clergy. Clergy become members of the General Synod through being elected as Proctors in Convocation. Each Archbishop is the President of his Convocation.

(b)   **The Church Assembly** came into existence as a result of the Enabling Act 1919. Before the passing of this Act the law affecting the Church could be altered only by Act of Parliament. The Church Assembly was a body composed of the two Convocations together with a House of Laity elected by the laity of the dioceses. It dealt primarily with administrative and financial matters, but it also possessed the legislative power, uniquely delegated to it by Parliament, to promote Measures.

6.2   The Archbishop of Canterbury and the Archbishop of York are joint Presidents of the Synod. The **General Synod** comprises three Houses. The House of Bishops (i.e. the Upper Houses of the two Convocations) consists of all the diocesan bishops, together with nine elected suffragan bishops. The House of Clergy (i.e. the Lower Houses of the two Convocations) consists of fifteen representatives elected by

61

the deans and provosts from among themselves, the Dean of Jersey or Guernsey, one representative archdeacon from each diocese, three service chaplains, the Chaplain-General of Prisons, six representatives of the clergy in the universities, two clergy representatives of religious communities, and proctors from each diocese elected by the clergy of the dioceses. The House of Laity consists of representatives from each diocese elected by the lay members of the deanery synods of those dioceses, three representatives of the lay members of religious communities and a few *ex officio* members. The General Synod in total comprises 566 members and elections are held every five years.

## The present position analysed

6.3 The General Synod has many critics. It is not unusual, for example, to read in the correspondence columns of the Church press strongly-worded attacks on the Synod, condemning it as unnecessary and costly, and blaming it for the damage caused to the Church (in the writer's eyes) by its decisions on controversial matters such as liturgical reform or the ordination of women. The tenor of the written evidence we received was quite different: it contained some generally-worded criticism of the system of synodical government as a whole – the Church is 'over-governed'; there are 'too many synods and committees' – but the need to retain the General Synod itself was unchallenged.

6.4 Synodical government is the subject of a separate review being conducted by a group under the chairmanship of one of our number, Lord Bridge of Harwich. We had the advantage of seeing some of the material produced for the Synodical Government Review Group, which will in turn address some of the issues raised with us (for example the frequency of General Synod meetings, the nature of the electorate for the House of Laity, and relationships between the General Synod and diocesan and deanery synods). Our concern is with the role of the General Synod within the national structures of our Church.

## The General Synod's functions

6.5 It is important to recall the functions of the General Synod as set out in Article 6 of its constitution, scheduled to the Synodical Government Measure 1969:

The functions of the General Synod shall be as follows:

(a) to consider matters concerning the Church of England and to make provision in respect thereof

(i)  by Measure intended to be given, in the manner prescribed by the Church of England Assembly (Powers) Act 1919, the force and effect of an Act of Parliament, or

(ii) by Canon made, promulged and executed in accordance with the like provisions and subject to the like restrictions and having the like legislative force as Canons heretofore made, promulged and executed by the Convocations of Canterbury and York, or

(iii) by such order, regulation or other subordinate instrument as may be authorised by Measure or Canon, or

(iv) by such Act of Synod, regulation or other instrument or proceeding as may be appropriate in cases where provision by or under a Measure or Canon is not required;

(b) to consider and express their opinion on any other matters of religious or public interest.

6.6    That Article describes the two functions of the General Synod. The first is to act as the Church of England's legislature, or in simpler terms its rule-making body; the second is to act as a national forum for the Church, to offer what one piece of written evidence described as a 'national shop-window'. We make some comment on each of these functions.

*Legislative and liturgical functions*

6.7    The language in which the Synod's legislative function is described in Article 6 is technical and reflects its history. The list in Article 6(a) of types of provision available to the Synod may be illustrated by reference to the legislation on the ordination of women to the priesthood. That involved two Measures, designed to have the force of Acts of Parliament (Article 6(a)(i)); two Canons adding to and amending the body of Canon Law (Article 6(a)(ii)); a set of Rules governing appeals on matters of financial provision (Article 6(a)(iii)); and an Act of Synod making arrangements for which a Measure or Canon was not required (Article 6(a)(iv)).

6.8    The creation of the General Synod twenty-five years ago gave the Church of England a single legislative body, possessing the power to pass Measures which Parliament had entrusted to the Church Assembly in 1919 and the ancient power of the (clerical) Convocations to make Canons. Both powers were now to be exercised by a body representative of bishops, clergy and laity. Such an assembly embodies the theological principle that underlies the whole of this report, that the Holy Spirit has been given to the Church as a whole. A report in 1902, *The Position of the Laity – The Report of the Joint Committee of the Convocation of Canterbury* (No. 367) (reprinted by the Church Information Board, 1953), put it in this way:

> The life and action of the Church [of the apostolic age] were the life and action of the whole body. The officers acted with, not instead of, the community; and the community acted with, not in mere obedience under, its officers.

The Church is thus neither democratic, nor despotic, but provides a practical way of embodying a 'corporate' or 'collective' life together.

6.9    The principle of consent to the law of societies was finely articulated by Richard Hooker at the end of the sixteenth century, specifically with reference to assemblies of representative persons: 'Laws they are not therefore which public approbation hath not made so' (*Laws of Ecclesiastical Polity, Book I, x, 8*). A combination of Parliament and the Convocations played this role in the early centuries of Anglican government, as became apparent when colonial circumstances compelled Anglicans to think out and develop structures of self-governance. The model of synodical governance shared by bishops, clergy and (male) laity appeared in the United States, and later in New Zealand, Australia and Canada, and by 1960 diocesan synods were a widely spread feature of Anglican experience. Bishop G A Selwyn, Bishop of New Zealand, for example, clearly believed in the 1840s that he was giving expression to the traditional Anglican ethos, in setting up a form of synodical government 'disencumbered of its earthly load of seats in Parliament, . . . compromises, corruption of patronage, confusion of orders, synodless bishops, and an unorganised clergy.' (William L Sachs, *The Transformation of Anglicanism*, CUP, 1993, p 191).

6.10    The subsequent (even belated) development of the General Synod within the Church of England was, therefore, not only a considerable simplification in the central structures, with the savings in time and money that that implied, but it was also a better expression of Anglican ecclesiology than the dual system which operated between 1920 and 1970.

6.11    We have no doubt as to the continued validity of the principles which led to the establishment of the General Synod as the Church's legislature. The Church must have a national body with power to deal with the legal rules which are to govern, and facilitate, its work. If it is to be true to itself, an Anglican church must incorporate within such a body the episcopal leadership of the Church, and representatives of the clergy and of the laity. Those elements must be present if decisions on matters of controversy, which may need to be settled by a legislative process, are to be acceptable as reflecting the mind of the Church. The General Synod's powers in respect of liturgy, which are derived from Measures and Canons, fall within this category.

6.12   It was not within the terms of reference of our Commission to address the relationship between General Synod and Parliament to which Article 6 makes reference. Nor are we concerned with those other Articles of the constitution which define the special role of the House of Bishops, or which require a special majority or the assent of a majority of the diocesan synods, in respect of certain types of decision. Those Articles are within the scope of the Synodical Government Review Group, though in Chapter 7 we consider the role of the House of Bishops more generally.

*Deliberative function*

6.13   The deliberative role of the General Synod, the power which Article 6 describes as 'to consider and express their opinion on any other matters of religious or public interest', is no less important than its legislative functions. Although some question the time spent by the Synod as a 'talking-shop', we believe that the Church needs a 'parliament' in the strict sense of that word: a forum in which leaders and representative members of the Church of England can reflect together and through which they can make the views of the Church known. The quality and style of many of the General Synod's debates has been the subject of a good deal of favourable public comment.

6.14   The expression of opinion, the declaration of the views of the Church, is only a part of a synod's deliberative function. Synods are an occasion for listening as well as for speaking, for learning from one another, for seeking together to know the mind of Christ. If a synod is one means by which the Church grows in understanding, it is not possible to measure its value simply by looking at its resolutions; and it is to be expected that its conclusions on difficult issues will sometimes have a tentative quality.

6.15   We would wish to affirm the continued importance of both the legislative and deliberative functions of the General Synod. Nothing in our recommendations would restrict or qualify the Synod's ability to discharge those functions; both are important, as is the ability of the Synod to use modes of procedure which vary with the nature of the task it is undertaking. We believe that the General Synod would benefit from the reforms we propose: a more coherent and responsive central structure would ensure that its debates and decisions were informed by clear and up-to-date policy analysis and information about resources.

*Appointments and cross-representation*

6.16   The analysis of the Synod's functions as legislative and deliberative omits two important features of current practice. One is the role of the

Synod in respect of appointments to positions of leadership in the Church and in the network of relationships between the official and voluntary bodies of the Church of England. This can be illustrated by a number of examples. Synod members themselves elect the officers of the Houses, the members of the Synod's Standing Committee and a part of the membership of its Boards and Councils (another part being appointed by the Appointments Sub-Committee of the Standing Committee). The Synod gives formal approval to certain appointments, notably that of the Chairman of the Central Board of Finance. Through its Crown Appointments Commission the Synod has a major influence on the appointment of diocesan bishops. Synod members are automatically members of diocesan and deanery synods, and in many dioceses are represented on the Bishop's Council. Some members are appointed to serve on the councils of theological colleges and courses.

6.17    Although the Synod is primarily an elected body, it contains within its membership almost all those charged with major tasks of individual or corporate leadership in the Church of England. All diocesan bishops are members of the House of Bishops, and the Synod also includes the three Church Estates Commissioners, the Chairman of the Central Board of Finance, the Chairman of the Pensions Board, and three senior ecclesiastical judges.

6.18    We think it important in any re-ordering of the Church's central structures to recognise the positive value of the features noted in the last two paragraphs. It is important that Synod members do not form a distinct legislative caste, but are fully involved in the local work of the Church and in other aspects of its life. And, while election gives to the Synod its essential legitimacy, the present structure recognises that contributions of expertise and experience can be made by people of real distinction who would never seek election as a diocesan representative, and who need to be brought into the central structures of the Church in other ways.

*Executive function*

6.19    Several of those who submitted written evidence argued that the General Synod is or should be the 'principal decision-making body on policy and resources'. This raises an important issue as to the extent of the General Synod's involvement in what, to use a secular analogy, we could describe as 'executive' decisions. The Synod is a legislature and national forum; the Church has its system of ecclesiastical courts and tribunals to discharge the judicial function; most of the issues we have had to address have been in the area of the executive function. Or, to use other language, if the Synod is the Church's parliament, who or where is its government? Can the Synod be a 'governing body' as well as a legislative and deliberative assembly?

6.20    We are properly cautious of secular analogies. Within a Christian community there should be little scope for fundamental differences between the leadership, however that is defined, and the wider member-ship; all share the same allegiance and mission. But as new issues present themselves or new circumstances arise, there can of course be disagree-ment as to the best approach. A Christian leader, like any other, must be prepared to argue his point of view, and be ready to reconsider if his view fails to win support. This is true at the parish level, in dioceses, and in the Church of England as a whole. At the national level, the General Synod represents the wider membership, and it is important to recognise that this and its legislative power, its control over 'the rules', gives it a special degree of authority.

6.21    Quite clearly an assembly of some 566 members, drawn from all over the country and meeting twice (or occasionally three times) a year, cannot be an executive body. As a representative assembly, it must be able to question, to seek and obtain information, and to express opinions which will influence, often decisively, the formation of policies. But it cannot itself be the forum in which those policies are formulated. The General Synod has its own role in governance: its legislation binds the Church, its resolutions influence Church opinion. It will often be invited to approve particular policy proposals. In terms of the central structures, however, its role is primarily reactive.

## The Synod's Standing Committee

6.22    The Standing Committee of the General Synod is sometimes represented, misrepresented we believe, as 'the Church's cabinet'. In the recent past it, and more particularly its Policy Committee, has tried to take responsibility for some strategic thinking on behalf of the Church, but the scope of this has been limited by the very fragmentation of the central structures which is a constant theme in our report.

6.23    The Standing Committee itself has 26 members, including both Archbishops and the Chairman of the Central Board of Finance, the balance being directly elected by the Houses of the Synod from among their membership. The chairmen of the major Synod Boards, usually bishops, also attend without the right to vote. It meets four times a year for some three to four hours on each occasion. Perhaps a third of its time is taken up with reviewing the business for the next group of sessions, so the time for general issues to be discussed is limited. Many would say that the Committee is too large for detailed discussion of issues, and that the election of its members as representatives of the variety of views within the Synod guarantees that it can never develop a sense of 'cabinet responsibility'.

6.24    *The General Synod Infrastructure Review: Report of the Review Officer and the Observations of the Review Group*, 1988, GS 827, presented a critical picture of the Committee:

> The Standing Committee has powers to determine priorities, to co-ordinate work done in the Synod's name and to give directions to Boards to modify or curtail their activities. But with the exception of BMU [the Board for Mission and Unity; the Committee took a keen interest in ecumenical debates] it has rarely exercised these responsibilities in the last 10 years. Contributory reasons have been:
>
> the Committee has not been responsible for advising the Synod about finance, thus weakening any impetus to tackle competing demands
>
> the Committee has taken the view that it should not interfere in a Board's work, especially over 'policy' matters
>
> the Standing Committee's agenda has been largely taken up by 'Synod business' . . . consequently the Policy Committee has never really focused on its responsibility for overall strategy and policy
>
> the size of the Standing Committee and the spectrum of views represented by its members make it an unsatisfactory forum for exercising control over the activities of the Boards and Councils. (paragraph 3.4, p 36f)

6.25    The Synod rejected one of the major recommendations arising out of the Infrastructure Review and designed to bring together policy and finance, the abolition of the Central Board of Finance. The Policy Committee of the Standing Committee has, however, sought to assume a larger role in strategic planning. It is a body of some twelve members drawn from the Standing Committee, with the First Church Estates Commissioner attending; it meets two or three times a year, often residentially. Its work is necessarily limited to the activities of the bodies responsible to the Synod, which restricts its ability to take an overview of the Church's needs. In financial matters, it co-operates with the Central Board of Finance in a Joint Budget Committee which shapes the annual Synod budget. Although the Church Commissioners are represented at meetings of the Policy Committee, their representatives often have to reserve the Commissioners' position on matters under discussion, pending consideration within the Commissioners' committees.

6.26    For the sake of completeness, it should be noted here that there are two other sub-committees of the Standing Committee, an Appointments Sub-Committee (which appoints Synod representatives on Boards and

Councils and some outside bodies, and which advises the Archbishops on some appointments they make as Presidents of the Synod) and a Business Sub-Committee (which plans the agenda for meetings of the Synod and keeps an eye on the way the Synod's business is conducted).

6.27    One of the groups which submitted written evidence argued that the Standing Committee had too much power in comparison with the Synod itself. This seems to us a misunderstanding of the different functions of the two bodies. The Standing Committee (with its sub-committees) has two types of work. One is essentially the preparation of the Synod's agenda and of the business to be considered, a facilitating role in which the Committee can give a lead but where the Synod has the right to take whatever decisions it thinks fit: what the Infrastructure Review referred to generally as 'Synod business'. That work will have to be done, whatever other changes are made as a result of our recommendations. The other is to carry out some 'central Church business', but here the fragmentation of the Church's central structures renders it incapable of seeing the whole picture, let alone taking firm decisions on any matter outside its immediate remit.

## The future

6.28    The National Council would provide, for the first time, a forum properly equipped to carry out the executive role in respect of central Church business. The Standing Committee and its Policy Committee have made valiant efforts to fulfil some of that role, but are unable to overcome the fragmentation of the Church's central structures. Their work in this respect would be absorbed into that of the Council, which would take over their functions. The work of the existing Boards and Councils of the General Synod would also be absorbed into the functions overseen by the Council, which would be able if appropriate to replace them in due course with more flexible structures to carry out, among other things, what we refer to in paragraph 6.27 above as 'central Church business'.

6.29    We propose that the Council should be a body corporate, drawing its authority from a Measure (an illustrative draft of which is at appendix B) passed by the General Synod. It would not be, in the technical sense, a 'subordinate body' of the General Synod created under the Synod's Standing Orders. It would, however, have a close relationship with the Synod, which requires careful explanation.

6.30    First, the membership of the Council would include the Archbishops and seven persons directly elected by the Synod or its

Houses and up to eight persons (including the Secretary General), whose nomination by the Archbishops for appointment to the Council would be subject to Synod approval. Second, all members of the Council would become members of the Synod, as, under present arrangements, are the officers mentioned in paragraph 6.17 above. Third, there would be a role for the Synod in furnishing many of those involved in the work of the Council. Fourth, the Synod would have total legislative control (subject to parliamentary approval) where the Council's proposals required legislation. Fifth, and perhaps most significant of all in practice, there would be an important measure of public accountability of the Council to the Synod, which (to repeat words already used) 'as a representative assembly . . . must be able to question, to seek and obtain information, and to express opinions which will influence, often decisively, the formation of policies' (paragraph 6.21). In chapter 7 we propose that the House of Bishops should develop a vision for the broad future direction of the Church. The Council would advise on the possible ways of translating it into action and on resources. These would be debated by the General Synod. We propose that a full report by the Council would form an important part of the business of the General Synod.

6.31    At the same time, the Council should be allowed to develop its own corporate style, strategy and impact, as a servant of the Church as a whole. It would be influenced by the vision of the House of Bishops and would present its overall plan and strategy to the General Synod for endorsement. In particular, the strength of the new Council would lie in its direct working relationship with the dioceses, especially on financial matters. This leadership role of the Council is crucial: we envisage that it would develop as it won the Church's confidence in its ability to take a clear strategic view of the Church's needs and priorities, and to secure the implementation of that view.

6.32    At present 'official' business (as opposed to private members' or diocesan synod motions) is introduced into the General Synod sometimes by the Church Commissioners but most usually by the Standing Committee, either on its own initiative or that of one of the Boards and Councils. This power would pass under our proposals to the National Council.

6.33    The Synod must be able to manage its own business. The precise ordering of its agenda, and the 'unofficial' business it chooses to consider, must be in its own hands. So too must the appointment of members to those committees charged with the conduct of particular pieces of business, such as steering and revision committees dealing with draft Measures.

6.34    In the new arrangements we propose, a **Business Committee** of the Synod would undertake the organisation and management of the meetings of the General Synod. We suggest that it should be under a duty among other things to make proper provision for the consideration by the General Synod of the business brought to it by the Council. Its chairman would be elected by the General Synod and it would have a majority of elected Synod members. The six officers of the Synod (the Archbishops, the Prolocutors and the chairman and vice-chairman of the House of Laity) would be *ex officio* members and there would be seven members (in addition to the chairman) elected by Synod (one bishop, three clergy and three laity elected by the members of the relevant House). The holder of the new post of Secretary General would also be a member. The overlap in membership between this important committee and the Council should ensure that the respective functions of each are well co-ordinated.

6.35    If the Commission's proposals were accepted, we envisage that the Synod would wish to appoint an **Appointments Committee** to assume the responsibilities of the present Appointments Sub-Committee of the Standing Committee. In addition to a chairman elected by the General Synod, the members of the Committee might, for example, be:

- five elected by the General Synod (one bishop, two clergy, two lay, elected by their respective Houses)

- two appointed by the Council

- the Secretary General.

6.36    In order to spread the representation of Synod members among these two committees we recommend that it should not be possible for members to be a member of more than one of them. This would be in line with the Synod's existing practice.

6.37    The Policy and Standing Committees would disappear. The relatively few statutory functions vested in the latter (some relating to the conduct of Synod business, others to the appointment of various Commissions and tribunals) would pass to the Business or Appointments Committees of the Synod or, in some cases, to the Council.

6.38    The Secretary-General of the General Synod is administrative head both of the General Synod Office, which provides the Synod's own secretariat, and of what is sometimes called the General Synod organisation, the Boards, Councils and other bodies working in or near Church House. The latter would fall within the national office of the Church of England under the Council, but the Synod would continue to need a secretariat. We do not think the holder of the new office of Secretary General should also be responsible for servicing the Synod. We propose the creation of a new office of Clerk of the Synod, responsible to the Synod. The Clerk would be appointed by the Synod for each synodical quinquennium on the recommendation of the Synod's officers. The Clerk would be responsible for administering the meetings of the General Synod and for servicing the Business and Appointments Committees, and would be assisted by a very small staff. Both the Clerk and staff would however be part of the staff of the national office.

6.39    An important element in the Synod's powers would be the consideration of the annual budget for national Church responsibilities: those central tasks funded by apportionment on the dioceses. We think it important that the Synod should retain control over this expenditure. In chapter 11 we make significant recommendations about meeting central costs from the budget for national Church responsibilities, which would bring a larger proportion of central costs under the scrutiny of the General Synod. In future, the budget would be prepared and presented to the Synod by the Council. The budget would be set out in the context of the financial plan for the Church as a whole, including expenditure on clergy stipends and pensions and all spending by the Council, whatever the funding source.

6.40    The General Synod would retain its distinctive role as a national legislative body. To some extent, the style and content of its legislation takes colour from the wider legal system within which it is set; and we reject the more extreme calls in some of the evidence we received for removal of the Church's legal system. Far from 'freeing the Church', that would subject its working wholly to the provisions of secular law. Within those limitations, however, we would look for Synod legislation that was less prescriptive and detailed, giving more discretion to dioceses and to those in day-to-day charge of various aspects of the Church's work to apply it in ways which best suit their local circumstances.

6.41    Throughout our report we stress the importance of ensuring that the work done by the central institutions is confined to only that which should be done at the national level and that it is done by as small an organisation as possible. We also stress the importance of ensuring that there are effective communications between the dioceses and the centre, and in that the relationship between the Council and the General Synod will play an important part. The current Review of Synodical Government chaired by Lord Bridge of Harwich may wish to consider whether our proposals have implications for the way in which the General Synod meets and works.

6.42    We have already explored the Bishop-in-Synod model as it relates to the structures we propose. We are convinced that the relationship we propose between the Council and General Synod would serve the Church well. The principles of synodical government would be fully protected, and indeed more coherently expressed. In its practical working, the Synod would be better informed, and be provided with a wider overview of the life of the Church and its financial and manpower needs.

# 7

# The House of Bishops and the Archbishops

## Background: the House of Bishops

7.1    The ancient Convocations of Canterbury and York each comprise an Upper House of Bishops and a Lower House of Clergy. The General Synod comprises these, merged into a single House of Bishops and a single House of Clergy, together with a House of Laity. Under Article 7 of the Constitution of the General Synod, 'a provision touching doctrinal formulae or the services or ceremonies of the Church of England or the administration of the Sacraments or sacred rites thereof shall, before it is finally approved by the General Synod, be referred to the House of Bishops, and shall be submitted for such final approval in terms proposed by the House of Bishops and not otherwise'. Thus on these subjects the bishops play a special role in the Synod's work.

7.2    The House of Bishops has twice yearly residential meetings. The Chairman is the Archbishop of Canterbury and the Vice-Chairman is the Archbishop of York, who also chairs its Standing Committee. At the meetings the bishops discuss a wide range of matters relating to the life of the Church. They also provide guidance to the Church and to the nation on Christian teaching and on moral and ethical issues. The meetings of the House of Bishops are serviced by the staff of the General Synod Office.

## The role of the House of Bishops

7.3    In chapter 8 (paragraphs 8.26 and 8.27) we reflect on the significance of the diocesan bishop and of the role of the bishop in diocesan and national life. In chapters 1 and 2 we set out the theological considerations which guided the formation of our proposals. These emphasise that within the Church of England the responsibility for keeping in view the goal or end of all things lies with the bishop in synodical association with the clergy and laity.

7.4    We believe the House of Bishops should in future play a more sharply focused and purposeful role among the national institutions of the Church. A key part of the role of the new National Council would be, under the guidance of the House of Bishops and subject to the strategic approval of the General Synod, to help the whole Church to develop its broad future direction. The Council would regularly seek the views of the House of Bishops on the priorities it proposes. The House of Bishops in turn would be able to ask the Council to take up and develop particular issues. Control of the business of the House of Bishops (and of the General Synod) would be with those bodies, although they would be serviced by the staff of the Council. We are proposing that the House of Bishops should elect two of its members to sit on the Council. They and the Archbishops and any other episcopal members of the Council would ensure (in consultation with the House of Bishops' Standing Committee) that the House developed, at regular intervals, an articulated vision for the direction of the Church of England. The General Synod would debate the vision and the House of Bishops would be informed by its views. The Council would advise on the possible ways of translating the vision into action and on the resources available to do so. The Church could thus forge the shared sense of direction and broad unity of purpose which some now feel it lacks.

7.5    The House of Bishops, in addition to exercising its primary role in relation to worship and doctrine, would continue to issue papers on matters of importance to the Church. It might also from time to time issue a pastoral letter. A more clearly focused and regular collective approach by the House of Bishops would not suppress openness of debate or differences of view within the Church. There are some matters – for example, in relation to worship and doctrine   on which it is of great importance to strive for an agreed collective view. There are others where differing opinions are valuable. The reflections of the bishops on the issues of policy and resources being handled by the Council would enrich the theological and intellectual quality of the debate on them in the Church as a whole.

7.6    It is appropriate for the House of Bishops to offer such vision and guidance because it is a college of chief pastors and has the responsibility for oversight (see paragraph 1.15). The bishops are best placed to propose broad directions because severally, and deriving from their oversight, they have the most general knowledge of their dioceses and thus, collegially, of the whole Church. But they would do so in consultation with the General Synod and the Council because the Church has a tradition of communal, as well as personal and collegial, *episcope* (see, again, paragraph 1.15). The tradition of obtaining the consent of the

75

Church recognises that the Holy Spirit distributes gifts to the whole Church. That forms the basis of the Church's legislation (see paragraph 6.8). It also recognises that the budgetary powers lie with the Synod.

7.7    The proposal that the House of Bishops should as one of its regular functions offer guidance on the overall direction of the Church would increase the demands placed on it. We therefore propose that the House should be properly supported in this role by the staff of the national office, which would also help to ensure effective links between the work of the House of Bishops, the Council and the General Synod. The staff would assist in the preparation and ordering of the business of the House and with following it through, and with the inspection of theological colleges. It is important that proper budgetary provision should be made for this support, so that the House of Bishops can adopt a new approach to its function. We doubt if it could be achieved as matters now stand with the load of business falling on the House of Bishops. We recommend that the new single staff service should support the House of Bishops in undertaking a radical review of its priorities, methods of working, agenda and resourcing.

7.8    The diocesan bishops already meet from time to time in regional groups. We propose in chapter 10 that these groupings should be standardised so that the same groupings are used by, for example, archdeacons and diocesan secretaries and others who meet on a regional basis. The House of Bishops on occasion uses these groups of bishops for the preliminary consideration of issues which come to the whole House. They might with advantage also use the groups to meet jointly with, for example, archdeacons or the chairmen of diocesan boards of finance to discuss certain issues. In considering the reordering of its business the House of Bishops should clarify the appropriate role for these regional groups, and for its own Standing Committee and Theological Group.

## Background: the Archbishops, Lambeth and Bishopthorpe

7.9    The Archbishop of Canterbury is Primate of All England and Metropolitan of the Province of Canterbury. He is also the highest ranking national figure after senior members of the Royal Family. He crowns the monarch, has a special relationship with the Royal Family, and is a member of the House of Lords. He is regarded as 'a vicar to the nation', articulating spiritual and moral guidance to the nation as a whole. A further dimension of this national role is his position as Patron or President of hundreds of national charities and schools.

He is Chairman of the Church Commissioners and, together with the Archbishop of York, a President of the General Synod.

7.10 The Archbishop of Canterbury is Diocesan Bishop of Canterbury. He is also spiritual leader of the 70 million strong Anglican Communion worldwide. The office of the Archbishop is key to the sense of identity of the Anglican Communion and to the capacity of its churches and their provinces to act and speak together. He is one of the world's prominent religious leaders with a special influence on relationships between Anglican and other Christian denominations and faiths around the world. Lambeth Palace handles pleas for intervention on behalf of vulnerable groups and individuals in every continent.

7.11 The Archbishop of York is Primate of England, Metropolitan of the Province of York, and Diocesan Bishop of York and has a substantial national role. He, too, is a member of the House of Lords. There is close teamwork and sharing out of tasks between the two Archbishops at international and national levels. On many issues the Archbishop of York can assume the leading role for the whole of the Church of England, not simply his own province. The Archbishops seek to ensure consistency, coherence and cross-fertilisation in the different parts of the Church, taking initiatives and where necessary setting up Archbishops' Commissions or other machinery to handle matters which straddle the responsibilities of separate Church bodies. They need to work in close partnership.

7.12 The Archbishop of Canterbury has a personal staff of around 40 comprising a Head of Staff and a Chaplain and Secretaries for Public Affairs, Press and Media, Anglican Communion Affairs, Ecumenical Affairs, and an Administrative Secretary together with support staff. The Church Commissioners meet in full the administrative expenses of Lambeth Palace which amounted to £732,000 in 1994. The Archbishop of York's office at Bishopthorpe is smaller, costing some £142,000 in 1994. Thirteen staff are employed in Lambeth Palace Library, the main library for the history of the Church of England. It is a national resource for the Church and is open to the public. Its administrative costs, which in 1994 were £103,000, are funded by the Church Commissioners.

# The Archbishops, Archbishops' staff and the Council

7.13 We have identified as a most important aim the exercise of more coherent leadership in those areas where decisions need to be taken at the national level. We believe that the two Archbishops, with their unique authority and prestige, should act as the fulcrum of the Bishop-in-Synod model embodied in the new arrangements if they are to work effectively. In addition to being Joint Presidents of the General Synod and chairing the House of Bishops, with its leadership role in relation to worship and doctrine and its overall vision for the Church, the Archbishops would also lead the new Council as Chairman and Vice-Chairman and be an important element in its authority.

7.14    At present, the widespread expectations placed on both the Archbishops as leaders within the Church of England take no account of the divisions between different components of the Church's national institutions and the lack of any coherent executive arm to complement the legislative and deliberative roles of the General Synod. In future, it should be easier for the Archbishops to lead.

7.15    There are of course limits to the Archbishops' capacity to take on new responsibilities. They would still have their very significant ministries to the nation as a whole, including to other national leaders, to the wider Anglican Communion, to the cause of ecumenical relationships in England and beyond and to their own dioceses. As Church of England Primates, much of what they alone can offer is brought to bear through teaching, preaching, officiating, pastoral care of brother bishops and many others, ambassadorial representations and the kind of personal encounters that can uniquely lift the spirits of individuals and groups within the Church and beyond. We do not seek to diminish these particular, multi-dimensional ministries, or to turn the Archbishops into businessmen.

7.16    We believe that, even within such a complex framework, the Archbishops can and will be personally engaged in the strategic leadership of the Church; and that this is particularly important in periods of change and tension. For example, it was so in handling the ordination of women to the priesthood and in the decisive response to the recent difficulties of the Church Commissioners, and it will certainly need to be so in future. Our analysis suggests that time already spent by the Archbishops in the existing separate bodies, in formal and informal meetings to hold the ring between them and weigh up their separate representations, would be spent much more effectively in leading the new Council and conferring between meetings with its members and senior staff. The chairmen of committees and other Council members should be able to relate to the Archbishops flexibly and sometimes frequently. The Archbishops in turn would rely on them and senior staff to involve them in matters genuinely requiring their attention but to get on with detailed management and day-to-day work within that framework.

7.17    We have carefully considered the implications of our main proposals for the organisation of the Archbishops' offices and their personal staff. It is far from simple to help the Archbishops exercise their wide ministries which extend beyond the organisational structures of the Church of England and yet also provide sustained leadership *within* them.

7.18    The inevitable difficulties are made worse by problems in combining the efforts of different central Church staff. For example, there is a physical and psychological divide between Lambeth Palace and Church House which makes it very difficult to bring to bear the combined wisdom and gifts of central Church staff in support of the Archbishop of Canterbury's ministry. Many Church House staff working to Synod Board agendas have only fitful contacts with the Archbishop and his staff and often feel remote from them. Moreover, the expertise and contacts of Church House staff are not as readily and flexibly available to the Archbishop's personal staff as they could be if all were working in the same place. They are at present different teams trying to co-operate with each other, rather than one big team serving one Church.

7.19    We recommend that the Archbishops' staff should be part of the unified staff service of the Church. Senior personal staff would, as now, be appointed by the Archbishops of Canterbury and York themselves from among both internal and external applicants, and their loyalty for the duration of their contracts would as now be unambiguously to the Archbishops. Given the unique and multi-dimensional character of the Archbishops' ministry, we do not doubt the continuing need for personal staff wholly dedicated to helping the Archbishops sustain their contributions and manage the complex demands on them. Staff numbers and roles should, however, be kept under careful review as the new arrangements develop. It would be important that there should be an established demarcation of the roles and tasks of the personal staff and their 'opposite numbers' in the staff of the Council.

7.20    We envisage that the Archbishops would both want and need to be frequently in the building in which the Council was based and to have offices of their own there. Given the bringing together of dispersed functions under one body and their key role within it, they would need to keep closely in touch, both formally and informally, with the rest of the Council and its staff. Moreover, we recommend that, so long as Lambeth Palace remains the Archbishop of Canterbury's headquarters, the new Council should sometimes meet there. This, too, would help counter any perception that the Council was a separate body which the Archbishop occasionally visited.

7.21   We have assumed that Lambeth Palace would remain the Archbishop of Canterbury's residence and the venue for his official receptions, entertainment and meetings, but we have considered whether most of the staff now working at Lambeth Palace should actually move to the national office. That could certainly improve joint working, and unlock new patterns of interaction and new creative energies. On the other hand, there is a strong 'family household' feeling about the Lambeth Palace team, and it is easy for the Archbishop to move flexibly in and out of 'work', 'family', 'meeting' and 'entertainment' mode, bringing these different aspects of his complex life together in a supportive atmosphere. To separate out his 'office' life would involve substantial disadvantages.

7.22   Moreover, great caution should be exercised before tampering with the historic and symbolic role of Lambeth Palace as the headquarters of the Archbishop of Canterbury. A proposal to move the Archbishop's office into the Council could arouse strong reactions from some bishops and others who for various reasons would not wish the See of Canterbury, with its national and international responsibilities, to become indistinguishable from the Church of England's central structures, or shrunk to a role analogous to 'Chairman of the Board'. There might be fears of 'capture' by the Secretary General and his or her colleagues. This reflects the fact that while to some the Lambeth Palace/ Church House divide seems mainly a source of frustration and incoherence, to others it enshrines part of the checks and balances through which the weight and prestige of the See of Canterbury requires a visible element of distinct-ness from other central Church bodies.

7.23   For these reasons, we believe that Lambeth Palace should continue to accommodate the Archbishop's personal staff. Naturally, collaborative working practices and good telecommunications can to some extent mitigate the effects of the physical and psychological divide. Indeed we believe that the Archbishops will wish to continue to reflect upon the long-term disposition and scale of their own staffs as the new national office and single staff service develops in practice. The processes through which greater coherence and more effective leadership are achieved may suggest further desirable changes and opportunities in due course, with the objective of encouraging the central structures of the Church to feel and behave as one body.

# 8

# The Church Commissioners

## Background: the Church Commissioners

8.1    The constitution of the Church Commissioners for England is set out in the Church Commissioners Measure 1947. The Measure incorporated the Commissioners with the purpose of uniting two pre-existing bodies: Queen Anne's Bounty and the Ecclesiastical Commissioners 'to promote the more efficient and economical administration of the Church of England'. In 1948 the property of these two bodies was vested in the Commissioners. The primary purpose of both Queen Anne's Bounty and the Ecclesiastical Commissioners may be summarised as providing financial assistance through the pay, pensions and housing of the stipendiary clergy of the Church of England. The Commissioners are in law a charity.

8.2    The original assets of Queen Anne's Bounty relate to the revenue from the First Fruits and Tenths which had been paid by the clergy to Rome before Henry VIII appropriated them, and which Queen Anne handed back to the Church in 1704. The collection of First Fruits and Tenths was abolished in 1926. At the time of amalgamation in 1948 the greater part of the assets of Queen Anne's Bounty was Government stock passed to Queen Anne's Bounty on the redemption of the tithe in 1936, and which was held for the benefit of more than 10,000 tithe-owning incumbents.

8.3    The assets of the Ecclesiastical Commissioners were accumulated under the extensive powers given to them in the nineteenth century. They were authorised to take over the endowments of certain sinecures and surplus offices, particularly in cathedrals. These endowments were used to create the common fund for making 'additional provision . . . for the cure of souls in parishes where such assistance is most required, in such manner as shall . . . be deemed most conducive to the efficiency of the Established Church' (Ecclesiastical Commissioners Act 1840, s.67). The Commissioners were also given power to take over some of the bishopric and dean and chapter estates. In return annual sums were secured to the bishop or dean and

and chapter, so the Commissioners' acquisition of these estates carried with them corresponding responsibilities. Nearly 40% of the total income of the cathedrals was diverted to the Ecclesiastical Commissioners in the mid-nineteenth century. Much of the Commissioners' current agricultural portfolio originates from the bishopric and dean and chapter estates. In 1954, £8 million was transferred from the Pensions Board to the Commissioners and clergy pensions became non-contributory and wholly charged on the Commissioners.

## The Church Commissioners' functions

8.4   The Church Commissioners' central responsibility is the investment of their inherited assets and the allocation of the income in support of the Church's ministry. This has included the continued development of the Commissioners' historic role in securing a more equitable distribution of resources among the parishes and dioceses of the Church, the identification of dioceses in special need and the targeting of funds. Other functions include their role as Central Stipends Authority; the exercise, in relation to benefice property and diocesan glebe, of a role similar to that exercised by the Charity Commissioners in relation to secular charities (with additional pastoral considerations); and carrying out various statutory duties in relation to proposals affecting parsonage houses and for pastoral reorganisation and the future of redundant churches; in particular they exercise an important role in considering representations concerning such proposals. Their many other administrative duties include the provision of stipends and housing for diocesan bishops and the payment of their expenses, the preparation of Parochial Fees Orders, providing financial assistance for new church buildings, the operation of the payroll covering 17,600 serving clergy and pensioners, and the compilation of *Crockford's Clerical Directory*.

8.5   The Commissioners' assets are invested primarily in Stock Exchange investments (45%) and property (54%) and their income applied mainly to clergy pay (37%), pensions (51%) and episcopal administration/payments to chapters (7%). The number of staff employed by the Commissioners in mid-1995 was 300, 35 of whom were on secondment to other Church organisations. Their asset management costs (£5.4 million in 1994) and their administration costs of central church functions (£5.4 million) are met from their investment income. In recent years they have also provided financial assistance towards the administrative costs of a number of other bodies, including the Church Urban Fund.

8.6    The composition of the ninety-five Church Commissioners is largely to be traced in the membership of their precursors. They comprise the Archbishops and forty-one diocesan bishops, the three Church Estates Commissioners, five deans or provosts, ten other clergy and ten laity (appointed by the General Synod), four lay people nominated by Her Majesty and four by the Archbishop of Canterbury, ten officers of State, four representatives of the cities of London and York and two of the Universities of Oxford and Cambridge. The full body of the Commissioners normally meets once a year to consider the Report and Accounts, to make appointments to the Board of Governors and to consider the allocation of available money.

8.7    The management of the Commissioners' affairs is in the hands of the Board of Governors and five committees plus a recently con-stituted Audit Committee. Subject to any general rules made by the Board, the Assets Committee by law has an exclusive power and duty to act in all matters relating to the management of assets, the income of which is carried into the General Fund, and to recommend what sums are available for application or distribution and what should be appropriated to reserve and for investment. The General Purposes Committee, which is also a statutory committee, recommends to the Board how available sums are distributed and considers other matters referred to it by the Board or not assigned to other committees. It also acts on behalf of the Board on staffing matters and any urgent business. There is a statutory Redundant Churches Committee. Remaining areas of the Commissioners' work are considered by the Pastoral and Houses Committees and a new Bishoprics Committee is being established which will assume some of the responsibilities of the Houses Committee, whose remaining functions are passing to the Pastoral Committee.

# The Church Commissioners and the need for change

8.8    In recent years the Church Commissioners made heavy financial losses and there were allegations that their financial management was flawed. Those events were thoroughly investigated by the Lambeth Group and the Church Commissioners accepted the Group's conclusions and have taken vigorous steps to implement its recommendations. The same events were also sharply criticised in a report produced in April 1995 by the House of Commons' Social Security Select Committee under the chairmanship of Mr Frank Field MP. The Archbishops established this Commission in the light of the Lambeth Group's recommendation that it would be appropriate for the Church to review its overall organisational structure in the light of its present day activities and requirements. Our concern therefore has been to review past events in a wider organisational context and to find appropriate structures for the future for financial management within the Church.

8.9    The main problem lies not so much with the Commissioners but with the arrangements in the Church as a whole for managing resources. The present pattern of the Church Commissioners' functions reflects their desire and their efforts over the years to meet the requests of the Church for help and support. The General Synod has made decisions about policy and, while the Commissioners have sought to provide the resources needed, it should have been clear to all that the resources available were not sufficient to sustain all the commitments entered into. The history of the Church Commissioners shows that throughout their existence they and their predecessor bodies accumulated a large number of responsibilities and functions in support of the Church. Some of these take the form of duties or obligations and some involve discretionary powers, although the Church Commissioners were not established as a body making policy for the Church as a whole. Indeed it is arguable that through spreading funds over all clergy (particularly through pensions) whilst retaining a (consequently) limited ability to focus funds strategically upon poor clergy and parishes and on mission areas, the Commissioners turned from a reforming charity into an agency which offered universal benefits to parishes and clergy (through flat-rate allocations and pensions), whilst still seeking to retain their original historic functions.

8.10    The support which the Church Commissioners have in the past been able to provide may have served to obscure the fact that the fundamental responsibility for the maintenance of the ministry rests with the bishop and his diocese. Some parts of the Church have perhaps expected too much from the central endowments. The reduction in the Church Commissioners' income has laid bare a need, which was always there, for the Church to find new endowments to finance its expenditure; and for it to take an overview of its total financial position. The likelihood is that a substantial proportion of the Commissioners' current capital assets will be earmarked or transferred to secure liabilities already entered into for the payment of clergy pensions. Some capital might have to be used to manage the important transitional phase during which dioceses assume responsibility for funding future pensions. Underlying all this is the large problem that, out of a desire to help the Church, the Commissioners have become committed to a level of expenditure which they cannot sustain without eroding their asset base.

# The National Council: implications for the Commissioners

8.11   Our proposal for a National Council makes it possible to look afresh at the role of the Church Commissioners. The new Council would have the responsibility of ensuring that an overview is taken of all policy and resource decisions in the Church so that the relationship between them is fully understood and that no commitments are entered into unless the resources are available to meet them. The new Council would be responsible for fostering between the parishes, the dioceses and the institutions at the national level a full understanding of the nature and extent of their respective responsibilities so that they worked in creative partnership for the good of the Church as a whole.

8.12   We believe the Church Commissioners should be retained as an independent trust as guardians and stewards of the centrally held historic assets of the Church (their 'core' function) but that their other functions should be transferred to the National Council. The Council, as the Church's central executive, could and should take on the many administrative functions which have fallen to the Church Commissioners by default. In future, decisions about spending the income which the Commissioners can make available from their assets should be made by the Council, on whose finance committee the diocesan boards of finance should be directly represented.

8.13   We did consider the option of recommending the abolition of the Church Commissioners, or the transfer of their functions to another of the central bodies. We do not, however, think it would be right for the capital of the central historic assets of the Church to be eroded or dispersed. Nor do we think it right for the Council to take on responsibility for the historic assets themselves. Recent events have demonstrated the prudence of ensuring that separate bodies are responsible for decisions about asset management and decisions about the expenditure of the income which the asset managers decide can be made available. We have had regard to the conditions on which the historic assets were originally accumulated at the centre and we respect them. The State has an interest in the origins of the assets, played a part in arranging for their surrender, and was the source of some of them. It is therefore appropriate that the assets should be managed by a body in which the historic partnership between the Church and the State continues to be embodied. We hope the State as well as the Church will find these reasons persuasive.

8.14    The Church Commissioners should remain as an important body which links Church and State in the affairs of the established Church. It is important not to lose sight of the theological imperative underlying the Commissioners' charitable function. The funds of Queen Anne's Bounty and the Ecclesiastical Commissioners had been used to alleviate genuine poverty among the clergy and their widows. The Church still faces a duty in charity to help those in need and that must continue to govern the way in which the income from the funds is deployed. It must also devote energy to finding equally imaginative and generous ways of alleviating the needs which will arise in the future, and for which the current generations of Church people are not making comparable provision.

8.15    The Church Commissioners would remain as trustees, embodying the historic partnership between Church and State in the guardianship of those historic assets which have been accumulated at the centre. Those assets would remain ring-fenced, so that neither the Commissioners nor any other body within the Church could spend the capital from them unless authorised by legislation to do so. The extent to which the income from the assets is already committed makes it rightly important that the funds are maintained in value and that in the longer term the capital is not eroded.

8.16    There would be a close working relationship between the Church Commissioners and the Council. In the past, the Commissioners have responded piecemeal to unconnected demands. In future, all demands would be mediated through the Council which would respond in the light of the amount the Commissioners could make available. The Commissioners, in turn, would be able in making their investments to take account of the Council's strategic view of the likely profile of the needs of the Church, but would also be free to undertake wider consultations of their own to inform the prudent discharge of their trustee responsibility. The Commissioners have a duty in law, which would remain, to hold a proper balance between the need for income and the preservation of the real value of the capital. The Commissioners would consult the Council, then decide and certify to the Council the amount of income to be made available to it. We consider that this clear demarcation of roles and responsibilities between the Commissioners and the Council would actually help the two bodies to work closely together. The likelihood is that, if the real capital value of the historic assets is to be maintained, the Commissioners would not be able to distribute on a regular basis in future as much of the income from the assets as they have distributed in the recent past.

8.17   Our recommendations (which we describe further below) would involve massive changes for the Church Commissioners. They would lose the majority of their functions; their composition would be totally changed, and their staff would be merged into the national office of the Church. Their funds are likely to be substantially reduced to meet the pensions commitments. Nevertheless, we believe that a radical refocusing on the Church Commissioners' core function would restore them to their appropriate place in the central structures of the Church. We note that this approach is in line with the recommendations of the House of Commons' Social Security Select Committee.

## The functions of the Council

8.18   Most of the Commissioners' functions would be transferred to the Council, together with all the legal obligations, duties, responsibilities and discretions entailed. The relevant statutes would be binding on the Council as they are now on the Commissioners. In relation to some functions (for example, the payment of the stipends of diocesan bishops, deans and provosts and two canons in every cathedral) there are corresponding charges on the Commissioners' assets. Those would remain. Unless and until the obligations were changed by law, the Council would discharge them. If it failed to do so, it would be breaking the law. Those functions would therefore be no less safe in the hands of the Council than they are now in the hands of the Church Commissioners. The key difference would be that the Council, as a policy body, would be in a position to look at the existing pattern of demands on the Commissioners' funds and to consider if they represented the best way of meeting the current requirements of the Church. To the extent that they did not, the Council would be able either to make adjustments where it had the administrative discretion or power to do so or to propose legislative changes to the General Synod. If legislation removed a function which had hitherto been financed by income from the Commissioners' funds, any money so freed could only (unless the terms of the trust were changed by legislation) be made available for the historic purposes of the cure of souls in parishes where it was most required. If any new expenditure were proposed, unless under legislation, the Commissioners would have to be satisfied that it fulfilled those historic purposes.

8.19   The Church Commissioners would require the Council to provide a certificate to the effect that the income made available had been spent in the discharge of all trusts and commitments to which the

Commissioners' income would have been subject, with the balance being made available for the cure of souls in parishes where it was most required. We see this as a check to ensure compliance, not as a detailed audit. The Council would, after all, like the Commissioners themselves, publish audited accounts and we envisage that in the course of a constructive working relationship the Commissioners would learn a great deal about the Council's work. Nevertheless, the compliance function must be real. We therefore propose that provision should be made by Measure for the Commissioners to require the Council to provide information on request about the actual purposes to which any of their income is put. Such a provision would also ensure that the Second Church Estates Commissioner continued to have the information needed to answer Questions in Parliament.

## Composition and status of the Church Commissioners

8.20   The Church Commissioners are a body corporate with certain statutory functions. In future the role of the Church Commissioners would essentially be to carry out the functions of the present Assets Committee and some of the trustee functions of the Board of Governors.

8.21   The proposed reduction in the ambit of the Church Commissioners' responsibilities (and considerations of economy) argue for a slimming down in the size of the body of Commissioners – there are currently 95 of them – and in the complexity of the current organisation. Our proposal, which we emphasise must be subject to discussion and agreement between Church and State, is that the number of Commissioners should be reduced to 15: the First and Second Church Estates Commissioners and three others appointed by the Crown, the two Archbishops, two bishops elected by the House of Bishops, a dean or provost, and two clergy and three lay members elected by the Houses of Clergy and Laity of the General Synod respectively. This broadly reflects the current balance between Church and State in the composition of the Commissioners. There would be no need for a separate Board of Governors or for a Third Commissioner. We have not consulted Ministers about our proposals for the representation of the State on the new Commissioners, or the non-Church bodies which appoint the present Commissioners (e.g. the ancient universities). This would be necessary before the changes were submitted for approval by Parliament.

8.22   The Commissioners would have a new Assets Committee. Its principal function would be to oversee the day-to-day management of the Commissioners' portfolio but it would not – unlike the present

Assets Committee – have exclusive power in all matters relating to the management of assets. The present structural arrangements have been much criticised and in future that power would lie with the Commissioners. The current arrangement secures an arm's length relationship between the body managing the assets and the body making decisions about the application of the income from them. In future that check would be secured by the division of functions between the Commissioners and the Council. What is important is to protect the body managing the assets from undue pressure to over-distribute. We think it important that there should be a specialist Assets Committee, which would include people appointed for their professional expertise, to advise the Commissioners. The Assets Committee would report directly to the Commissioners and its membership would include Commissioners. An Audit Committee would, with the assistance of the Commissioners' external auditors, scrutinise annually all aspects of the work of the Commissioners and of the Assets Committee and report to the Commissioners. The Comptroller and Auditor General or any appointed firm of independent auditors would continue to report on the accounts of the Commissioners before they were laid before Parliament.

8.23    The Commissioners would, as now, be required to report both to the General Synod and to Parliament. Members of both bodies would continue to be able to ask questions: in the case of the Synod this would be pursuant to Standing Orders, and the First (or, now, Third) Commissioner answers; in the case of Parliament, the Commissioners are constitutionally bound to answer Parliamentary Questions, and the Second Commissioner does so in the House of Commons. By convention he also steers Church legislation on the Synod's behalf through the House of Commons. In addition the Commissioners are required by statute to submit their Annual Report and Accounts to the Home Secretary and Secretary-General, to be laid before Parliament and General Synod respectively. These arrangements would continue.

## The support of bishops

8.24    The Archbishops and bishops are supported by the Church Commissioners under the Episcopal Endowment and Stipends Measure 1943. The stipends of the Archbishops and three historically senior diocesan bishops are settled by the Church Commissioners after consultation with the Archbishops. The 1943 legislation also empowered the Commissioners to pay such expenses as they consider it necessary for the bishops to incur. In the last decade or so funds have also been provided for suffragans' expenses on a discretionary basis.

8.25    In 1972 the General Synod established a Central Stipends Authority for the Church of England and appointed the Church Commissioners to be the Central Stipends Authority. The Central Stipends Authority Regulation 1982 stipulates that the Central Stipends Authority shall keep under review and adjust as appropriate the stipends of diocesan bishops, deans, provosts and residentiary canons and the augmentation of suffragan and assistant bishops and archdeacons. We propose that the new Council should assume the responsibilities of the Central Stipends Authority.

8.26    Bishops are nominated by the Crown for formal election by Cathedral Chapters. They swear allegiance to the Sovereign and take an Oath of Obedience to their Archbishop. They do not formally answer to anybody within Church or State for the discharge of their ministry although there is a *de facto* accountability to their own Bishop's Council, their diocesan synod, the House of Bishops and the Archbishops. The two Archbishops and the Bishop of London are members of the Privy Council; and they and other senior diocesan bishops are members of the House of Lords. Both the Church and the nation make heavy demands on all diocesan bishops and have high expectations of them. They occupy a distinctive place, both constitutionally and by custom, within the civic and political life of the nation. They have a unique opportunity to move naturally across the boundaries of Church and State and in this their traditional independence is an asset.

8.27    The distinctive characteristics of the role of the diocesan bishop make it vital that the high degree of independence which is essential to their functions is safeguarded within the central structures and in the arrangements made for their support. Their independence is one of the distinctive features of the dispersal of authority in the Church of England. The significance of the role of the bishop in the Church is set out more fully in chapter 1. The distinctive characteristics which attach to the role of diocesan bishop relate principally to his jurisdiction within his diocese and to his national role. Diocesan bishops must be free from improper pressure from those they oversee and those to whom they minister.

8.28    There is no hierarchy of order in the episcopal ministry, but the characteristics of the diocesan bishop's role do not attach to suffragan bishops in the same way. The only small distinction we make – and it does not bear on the nature of episcopacy – is to propose that all the costs of supporting suffragan bishops should in future be borne by the dioceses. The cost of housing suffragan bishops has long been a responsibility of the dioceses, although the Commissioners have from time to time been able to make grants and loans to help meet the cost. Moreover, the Commissioners only quite recently assumed responsibility for funding the expenses of suffragan bishops. We see no compelling argument for these to continue to be borne centrally, nor do we believe there is a strong rationale for the existing distinction between the housing and other forms of financial support of suffragan bishops. Our recommendation is consistent with the approach to central costs which we set out in chapter 11. We do not, however, regard it as a first order issue or one which affects our key recommendations.

8.29   We are keenly aware of the need to ensure that no function is carried out by the national bodies of the Church which can more appropriately be carried out in the dioceses. We have therefore considered very carefully the arguments in favour of transferring the support of diocesan bishops to the dioceses. Some dioceses are known to favour such an arrangement, feeling that it would introduce greater account-ability and enable the resource issues to be settled in a local diocesan context. The main financial argument is that it would leave the Commissioners with a stronger allocation capacity for the needier parishes and dioceses. Nevertheless, we think it right that the arrange-ments for support should secure the independence of the diocesan bishops, given their standing in national life and their role in the Church. Just as clergy stipend levels are in general not determined by individual parishes but are set within broad guidelines agreed nationally, so decisions about the support of bishops should be made at some level beyond the local and in a context wider than the diocese.

8.30   The assets of the Church Commissioners include the episcopal property vested in them by the Episcopal Endowments and Stipends Measure 1943. These originally belonged to the bishops but now form part of the historic assets of the Church. It is appropriate that the Church Commissioners, as trustees and as a body on which the State is represented, should continue to own those assets on behalf of the Church as a whole. It is proposed that the cost of the improvement, repair and maintenance of the Archbishops' palaces and diocesan bishops' see houses should continue to be met from the Commissioners' funds within a budget proposed by the Council. These buildings serve also as offices and some provide staff accommodation; the salaries and pensions of diocesan bishops' support staff and episcopal expenses should also be met from the Commissioners' income.

8.31   We recommend that a Bishoprics Committee should be estab-lished. It would operate within the Council structure, but its members would be appointed by the Church Commissioners and the Council and it would be a joint committee of both bodies. Since the bishops are national as well as ecclesiastical figures, the Church Commissioners as a body in which both Church and State play a part should be involved. At the same time, we do not wish to erode the key principle that the Council should have an overview of the policy and resources of the Church as a whole, and we wish to ensure that decisions about the level of support given to bishops are made in the context of the whole budget. The Bishoprics Committee would have ten members, five nominated by the Church Commissioners and five by the Council. Its membership would include at least two bishops, two clergy and two lay people.

8.32    The budget for the stipends, expenses and housing of bishops would be set by the Council in consultation with the Bishoprics Committee. The consultation process would enable the Church Commissioners, through their membership of the Committee, to express a view on whether the level of support proposed was appropriate within the terms of the Episcopal Endowment and Stipends Measure 1943. The Church Commissioners would be able to ensure that the arrangements made for the expenditure of income were in accordance with the purposes of their historic trusts. The Council, for its part, would bring to the Committee a wider perspective which would enable it to place the expenditure on the support of bishops in the context of the other demands on the Church's finances and where necessary propose economies. The Bishoprics Committee would oversee the administration of episcopal support, which would be carried out by the central staff, including the maintenance of the see houses. The size of the overall budget for this function (but not the detail of how it was administered) would be set out for the General Synod by the Council.

8.33    The Council should at an early stage open consultations with the dioceses about transferring to them the responsibility for paying the stipends and expenses of suffragan bishops (though their stipends would continue to be set centrally). Although not a key issue, we see this as an important part of the general move towards the goal of the centre and the dioceses sharing responsibility for a wide range of issues and deciding on them in consultation with each other. The question whether a diocese needs a suffragan bishop – or more than one – is a matter for debate between the diocese and the national Church and it is right that the costs should feature in the debate. We recommend (see paragraph 10.16) that the provisions of the Dioceses Measure 1978 should be changed so that the Dioceses Commission has the power to initiate reviews of such matters of diocesan organisation.

# Cathedrals

8.34   Cathedrals play a crucial part in the life and mission of the Church of England, as was recognised and affirmed by the Archbishops' Commission on Cathedrals, which published its report, *Heritage and Renewal,* in 1994. The Deans or Provosts in Convocation are non-diocesan members of the General Synod. Under the Cathedrals Measure 1963, the Church Commissioners pay the stipends of the dean or provost and two residentiary canons of each cathedral. The Commissioners also have certain powers in relation to the inspection and repair of cathedrals and make grants, on behalf of chapters, to cover cathedrals' liability for the chancels of about two hundred parish churches. They are technically liable for the employers' National Insurance on cathedral stipends, although the cost is now refunded by cathedrals.

8.35   The Commissioners also make grants, under section 31 of the Measure, to help fund other cathedral clergy stipends and lay salaries. Grants are increasingly being targeted towards the poorer cathedrals for whom they often represent a substantial proportion of their expenditure. In 1993, five cathedrals received over 50% of their income from a section 31 grant, whilst the wealthiest cathedrals receive no grant. The Church Commissioners' support of cathedrals in 1995 will be approximately £2.2 million for the stipends of deans or provosts and two canons in each cathedral and £2.7 million for section 31 grants, a total of £4.9 million.

8.36   We recommend that support for cathedrals should continue to be provided from the Church Commissioners' income, not least in recognition that the Commissioners' assets derive in part from the dean and chapter estates transferred to the Ecclesiastical Commissioners in the nineteenth century. The stipends of cathedral clergy would be set by the Council as the new Central Stipends Authority. The Council would, as described in paragraph 8.18 above, assume responsibility for the payment of the stipends of deans and provosts and two canons in every cathedral. Responsibility for the payment of grants under the Cathedrals Measure 1963 for the maintenance or repair of cathedral clergy houses and towards the stipends and salaries of cathedral clergy and staff would be transferred to the Council, as would the functions of the Church Commissioners in relation to cathedral land, funds and the inspection and repair of cathedrals. We believe that the transfer of these functions would enable the work and mission of cathedrals to be seen in the context of, and debated alongside, the other priorities of the Church in its ministry and mission to the nation.

# Other liabilities

8.37 The Church Commissioners now lend capital to the Church by way of mortgages and loans which currently have a total capital value of £200 million. The funding for such loans would in future be a matter for negotiation between the Council and the Commissioners (or the Council and the trustees of the pension fund). It would be for them ultimately to decide what sums they were willing to make available to the Council and on what terms. The Council would administer any mortgages and loans and determine the policy governing them. The Commissioners would under our proposals be solely responsible for decisions about the investment of their assets and would normally expect to make all loans available at a commercial rate. It would therefore become a matter for the Church as a whole to decide if it wished to charge the recipients of the loans a lesser amount, and how the cost of any such subsidy could be met. The question of how transitional and future provision for these mortgages and loans would be made serves to expose the realities of the financial issues facing the Church, as does the question of paying central costs, which is dealt with in chapter 11. Transparency and openness require that such hitherto hidden subsidies should be recognised explicitly and paid for by the dioceses and this is an issue which the Council would have to discuss with the dioceses and with the Commissioners at an early stage.

# Legal provisions

8.38 The Church Commissioners would in future have only the following principal functions:

- determination and monitoring of asset and investment policy (including ethical issues)

- ownership and management of the Stock Exchange portfolio

- ownership and management of the commercial, residential and agricultural portfolios

- administration of the Property Pool on behalf of dioceses and chapters which wish to invest in it

- holding of diocesan pastoral accounts and diocesan stipends fund capital accounts (until transferred to dioceses)

- jointly with the Council, the support of diocesan bishops, including ownership and management of see houses

- providing financial projections of the Commissioners' income and deciding and certifying to the Council the amount of income to be made available

- obtaining a certificate from the Council that the income has been spent in accordance with the historic trusts.

8.39   The following functions would be transferred from the Church Commissioners to the new Council and its supporting structures:

- allocation of the income provided by the Commissioners

- grants towards cathedrals, clergy housing and towards other bodies such as the Church Urban Fund

- jointly with the Church Commissioners, the support of diocesan bishops

- work currently undertaken by the Commissioners as Central Stipends Authority, including decisions about the level of stipends

- operation of the clergy payroll (and the compilation of *Crockford's Clerical Directory*) and maintenance of diocesan stipends fund income accounts

- functions under the Cathedrals Measure 1963

- approval of the acquisition, disposal and improvement of parsonage houses (many of the functions in relation to which are to be transferred to the dioceses) and the consideration of representations

- approval of glebe sales and the consideration of representations against proposed sales

- administration of grants and loans

- casework and policy issues arising from the Pastoral Measure 1983, including issuing draft schemes and the consideration of representations.

The Pastoral Measure provides that the Commissioners shall appoint a Committee for the carrying out of their statutory functions; a majority of the Committee must be Commissioners. This obligation would pass to the Council, and comparable arrangements would have to be made to ensure that this important area of work was properly given arm's length supervision acceptable to other interests, in particular the State.

8.40   The changes which we propose in this chapter would require consultation with the State and legislation by way of Measure. An illustrative draft of such a Measure is set out in appendix B.

# 9

# The Pensions Board

## Background: the Pensions Board

9.1 The Pensions Board was established by the Clergy Pensions Measure 1926 to serve as the pensions authority for the Church of England and to administer a comprehensive pension scheme for the clergy. The Board was given powers in 1948 to provide housing for retired clergy and their widows and widowers. The Board is also corporate trustee of four other pension schemes including two through which over 70 Church organisations make pension provision for their lay employees, and a total of ten charitable funds. The Board is directly accountable to the General Synod.

9.2 The Board consists of twenty-two members of whom the Chairman and sixteen others are appointed by the General Synod and five by the Church Commissioners (one of whom must be a diocesan bishop). The management of the Board's affairs is shared between three standing committees – the General Purposes Committee, the Housing and Residential Care Committee and the Investments and Finance Committee. The board's fifty-five administrative staff are based at 7 Little College Street (part of the Church Commissioners' building at 1 Millbank) in Westminster. As a result of the same 1954 legislation that transferred responsibility for the cost of clergy pensions, the Board's administrative expenses, which in 1994 amounted to £1.8 million, are met by the Church Commissioners. A report to the General Synod in 1984 recommended that the two bodies should be merged, but the motion was defeated.

9.3 In 1954 it was decided that the cost of clergy pensions should be made a statutory charge on the Commissioners' investment income, the assets of the then separate pension fund being transferred to the Commissioners, and that clergy should no longer have to contribute towards the cost of pensions. The Pensions Board and the Church Commissioners work together on clergy pensions and retirement housing issues and have jointly submitted a number of reports to General Synod. The current package of pensions and related benefits derives mainly from a joint paper approved by the General Synod in 1980 and the implementation during the 1980s of the aspirations contained in that paper. The policy was reaffirmed by the Synod in 1991.

9.4    The Board provides from its own funds some 500 retirement properties and mortgage loans. In order to meet the increasing need for such housing assistance the Board began, at the end of the 1970s, to borrow capital from the Commissioners. The current scheme administered by the Board – the Church's Housing Assistance for the Retired Ministry – was established in 1983 with the approval of the Synod. The Commissioners now make available from their capital the funds necessary to finance almost all new mortgage loans and rented property made available to retired clergy and widows. A total of some 3,200 pensioners are currently taking advantage of the scheme. In addition, the Board owns and manages eight residential homes and one nursing home, the cost being met both from fees and from the Board's charitable resources. At the end of 1994 there were 10,800 pensioners, including 4,250 widows. The Commissioners also provide from their income a subsidy to ensure that no participant in the retirement housing scheme has to pay more than 25% of their total income for housing. The cost of this was £1.2 million in 1994.

## A clergy pensions fund

9.5    There remains little scope for continuing to meet the whole of the cost of clergy retirement benefits in the same way as in the past, and major discussions have been held between the Church Commissioners, the Pensions Board, the Central Board of Finance and the dioceses to see how pension cover can be provided for the future. A number of options are being discussed, but they all have the common feature that they will for the first time require significant contributions from the dioceses. A newly established pension fund will receive pension contributions for future service from the dioceses and, subject to further discussions, a capital transfer from the Commissioners in respect of past service is likely to be made if this proves the best way of discharging that liability.

9.6    Parliamentary legislation on pension funds generally is likely in the near future to require pension schemes to follow recommendations made in the Goode Report that both the sponsors and the members of a pension scheme should be represented on its governing body. The 'members' are the beneficiaries – the clergy and lay workers – under the various Church pension schemes. The Goode Report recommended that

97

representatives of the members of the schemes should make up at least one third of the trustee body; the remainder should represent the sponsors.

9.7    Although it is clear who are the 'sponsors' under the schemes for lay workers, it will be necessary to decide who, for these purposes, should be the sponsor of the new fund for clergy. In a commercial company, the sponsor would normally be the employer. In the Church a number of bodies share the responsibilities and concerns about clergy pensions which would normally fall to a single body. In future, each of the forty-three mainland dioceses will have a new and very significant responsibility for providing contributions towards clergy pensions. The General Synod will remain concerned to see that adequate pensions are provided. The Church Commissioners may for some time continue to be financially involved, though in ways and in amounts yet to be decided.

9.8    At the heart of our recommendations is the key proposal that policy and resource matters should be considered together so that when-ever a decision of policy is made it is only after the implications have been fully explored with those who would be responsible for finding the resources to implement it. It will be important in future that the dioceses are closely involved and are represented on the governing body of the clergy pensions fund. Given the role and composition of the Council (see chapter 5), it is proposed that the best means of securing this is to nominate it as the sponsor of that scheme. The Council would act as a proxy for what, in a commercial company, would be the employer. The Council would have responsibility for clergy pensions policy, formulating proposals on the shape of the benefits package, the level of pensions increases, and on contributions to fund the arrangements. In formulating its proposals the Council would need to consult very closely with the dioceses.

## The trustee body

9.9    The Council, as sponsor, would be able to consider the whole question of clergy retirement provisions as part of the total costs of ministry, the other main elements of which are stipends, National Insurance and housing. (It is for this reason that we suggest the Council might have a resources for ministry committee which would draw together these questions.) As described above, the Council would, on pensions issues, formulate its proposals in very close consultation with the dioceses and the trustees of the clergy pension scheme.

9.10   The trustees of a pension fund are not policy makers; they are guardians of the arrangements, managing the assets and paying benefits within terms established by the sponsor. We believe the same body of pension trustees should administer the new clergy pension scheme and all the existing schemes and charitable funds administered by the Pensions Board, and advise on costs and on aspects of how the schemes operate. They would decide how the rules of the schemes are applied in individual cases.

9.11   We propose that the Pensions Board should be reconstituted on the lines recommended in the Goode Report and that the new pensions trust might have fifteen trustees, with the one-third representing the members of the various pension schemes being made up of one bishop elected by the House of Bishops, one representative lay employee, and three clergy (two from the Province of Canterbury and one from the Province of York) elected by the House of Clergy of the General Synod. The trustees appointed by the sponsors would need to reflect the balance from time to time between the various bodies which are funding contributions to pensions. There would be a chairman, who would either be a senior member of the Council's representatives as sponsor or a person nominated by the Council and endorsed by the General Synod, and three other members appointed by the Council. In addition, six diocesan representatives might be appointed by the Council after discussion with the dioceses through the six proposed regional groupings (see chapter 10).

9.12   We believe that there should be a department within the national office responsible for all those matters currently administered by the Pensions Board. We do not believe that the trustees of the new pensions fund should have day-to-day responsibility for these matters. We see no reason for the new pensions fund to consider (or to pay for) matters other than those that would be within the remit of a pensions fund in industry. We believe that the pensions payroll, the administration of the housing schemes and the employment of all members of the Board's staff should be in the hands of the Council. Nonetheless, they would all be under one roof and we believe that a 'one-stop service' for prospective pensioners still should and could be provided. We recognise that this would result in the majority of the Board's costs transferring to the Council with a consequent increase in the apportionment on dioceses of around £1.5 million. We discuss the implications of this further in chapter 11.

# 10

# The dioceses

## Background: the dioceses

10.1 The Church of England comprises forty-four dioceses, each under the oversight of a diocesan bishop, assisted by suffragan or assistant bishops, archdeacons and other senior staff. A diocesan office typically provides the focus for most of the administration required at diocesan level and provides a link with the national institutions. Clergy and lay people generally turn to their diocesan office on any matters that extend beyond the jurisdiction of the parish.

10.2 Each diocese has a diocesan synod presided over by the diocesan bishop and comprising a House of Bishops, a House of Clergy and a House of Laity. The diocesan synod considers matters concerning the Church of England and makes provision for them in relation to the diocese. It advises the bishop on any matter on which he may consult the synod; it deals with matters referred to it by the General Synod and can also refer matters to the General Synod. The synod makes provision for the financing of the diocese. Every diocesan synod must establish a Bishop's Council, whose membership is specified by the standing orders of that synod. The Council advises the bishop and acts as the standing committee of the diocesan synod.

10.3 In addition to the Bishop's Council and Standing Committee and the Diocesan Board of Finance (a charitable limited company), each diocese has a number of statutory boards and committees. A Diocesan Parsonages Board is a body corporate with power to enter into contracts, hold property, borrow money and execute works. Each diocesan synod must also appoint a Pastoral Committee (which considers proposals for pastoral reorganisation in the diocese, and which may in turn set up deanery or archdeaconry pastoral committees), a Redundant Churches Uses Committee (charged with finding appropriate uses for redundant churches), a Diocesan Education Board, a Diocesan Advisory Committee for the Care of Churches and a Glebe Committee.

10.4 There is also a wide variety of non-statutory boards and committees in each diocese dealing with such matters as training and ministry, readers, youth work, social responsibility and Christian stewardship. There is a great diversity as far as non-statutory boards are concerned in terms both of the number of boards and of the number of staff employed in each of these areas. Several dioceses are currently re-considering their board structure.

## The relationship between the dioceses and the national Church

10.5 Although the Commission's terms of reference invited it to examine the functions of the national institutions of the Church, the way in which those institutions affect the life of the dioceses (and in turn the parishes), and the relationship between them and the dioceses, have a bearing on what the centre itself does. Our examination of the national level of the Church has served to underline the great importance of the diocese in the organisation of the Church. A national Church will always need to undertake certain tasks centrally and we set out our views on this in chapter 3 (from paragraph 3.31 onwards). However, the balance between the national level and the dioceses may change over time, for example, as the dioceses' reliance on income from the central historic resources declines as a proportion of their overall expenditure. This important shift of financial responsibility needs to be recognised.

10.6 The National Council would have to be rigorous in ensuring that functions were performed at the centre only where that was the most appropriate level. The dioceses already elect virtually all of the representatives of the General Synod and one of each diocese's representatives is a member of the Central Board of Finance. Nevertheless, we find that this representation has not proved an effective means of communicating the financial concerns of the diocesan boards of finance, or provided sufficiently clear representation for dioceses in the areas of policy making and resource direction. We therefore recommend that the membership of the finance committee of the proposed Council should include six DBF chairmen, one elected by each of the six regional groupings which we propose later in this chapter. We hope the episcopal, clergy and lay representatives of the dioceses on the General Synod will consider the implications of this recommendation. The evidence we have received has disclosed a concern that considerations of churchmanship feature too prominently in General Synod and that members may not sufficiently reflect the concerns of their particular dioceses. It is clear that the dioceses would also like their representatives to convey their concerns about resources and policy but have no formal role in briefing them. In view of the General Synod's important role in relation to the financial apportionment on dioceses, and the increase we propose in the use of apportionment to fund the national functions of the Church, the dioceses should consider carefully the extent to which they brief their elected members on the financial and other implications for them of the General Synod's work.

10.7   We believe it is essential that the dioceses and the central institutions should develop an improved relationship and an open sharing of information. There needs to be a clear understanding of the issues being discussed by different bodies within the Church. We believe that mutual trust can and will emerge from such a partnership. The dioceses and the bodies at the national level must see themselves as complementary and be ready to transfer information and functions between them or to such other levels (the region, deanery or the parish) as seems from time to time to be appropriate in each instance.

10.8   We hope the Council will place great emphasis on improving communications by the spoken and printed word and through information technology and telecommunications. It should communicate information about the national financial situation of the Church in a standard format which allows local information to be added in a way which shows how it fits into the whole and makes transparent the way in which the giving of the local church is spent. This information should be communicated widely by all appropriate means, for example, posters, pew leaflets and diocesan newsletters. We propose that the Council should take an overview of the policy and resource issues facing the Church as a whole and propose strategies for dealing with them. These will be effective only if they are well understood at all levels in the Church. It will be important for every diocese to give clergy and laity opportunities to discuss the Church's strategies and feel fully involved in implementing them. While it is not our task to make recommendations about diocesan or deanery synods, dioceses may well feel that large conferences would help in communications with the parishes.

10.9   We have been particularly stimulated by – and agree with – the theological insights set out in *A Fresh Start* (The Report of the Birmingham Diocesan Structures Review Commission, 1991). The Church is an embodiment of the presence of God and the Church as an institution should not be separated from the Church as a community.

We are reminded in Ephesians 2.20-21 that Jesus Christ is the Church's cornerstone 'in whom the whole structure is joined together and grows into a holy temple in the Lord'. Institutions can of course go terribly wrong but they are essential to life and have to be shaped and re-shaped, looking to God for wisdom. We have emphasised throughout our report the importance of becoming aware of God and his purposes and of being a learning Church, willing to grow and to change. The principal purpose of diocesan structures is to support and help to build up the key aspects of Church life: worship, service and witness. Much of this will be done by parishes but episcopal oversight is essential if the bishops, clergy and people of the diocese are to work as one body.

10.10 Dioceses require appropriate structures to enable the mission and ministry of the Church to be exercised as effectively and efficiently as possible within their geographical area. All dioceses need boards and committees which can ensure that issues such as finance, pastoral reorganisation and education are fully considered. However, we believe that a degree of flexibility is necessary to allow dioceses to develop a board structure which they feel is appropriate. There are considerable variations between the dioceses, for example in size and sociological and demographic composition, and we favour over time some relaxation of the statutory framework which governs diocesan administration.

10.11 We commend to dioceses the spirit of our recommendations about the national level, especially where we recommend that the size of many boards should be reduced, that staff should be given greater executive authority (and be held accountable for it) and that a greater reliance should be placed on *ad hoc* working groups comprising members selected for their expertise. We encourage dioceses to adopt a constructive approach to any such changes at the national level and to consider how they might apply these principles to their own structures. We hope they and the Council will share in the dissemination of good practice. Dioceses must be rigorous in ensuring that their structures and their administration are, and remain, as effective and efficient as possible. There is considerable scope within existing legislation to make changes – and we are aware that some dioceses are already taking advantage of this – and we hope that a partnership with the national level will develop which will facilitate the passage of legislation to allow greater flexibility in certain areas currently regulated by statute.

10.12 Dioceses are responsible for the administration of many funds and assets and we support the current proposal that diocesan pastoral accounts, diocesan stipends fund capital accounts and parsonage building funds should pass from the Church Commissioners to dioceses. We believe that dioceses would be well able to manage these additional responsibilities without additional staff. A number of functions – the clergy payroll, for example – are carried out centrally purely for reasons of cost effectiveness. Once the new overall structures which we propose were in place, it would be open to dioceses from time to time to suggest realignments of responsibilities between the national level and dioceses. Indeed, the principle of subsidiarity which we encourage requires that the dioceses satisfy themselves that they could not themselves perform more efficiently some of the tasks which are done by the national institutions.

## Regional groups

10.13 There are regional groupings within the Church of England for bishops, archdeacons, DBF chairmen, diocesan secretaries, diocesan communications officers, diocesan stewardship officers and urban priority area link officers. These regional groupings have evolved or been devised independently of each other and have never been standardised. For example, the bishops in one diocese might belong to one grouping, the archdeacons to another and the diocesan secretary to yet another. We see considerable value in these groupings, both for pastoral support and to discuss issues with local colleagues, but agree with those who have suggested to us that the groupings would be more effective if they were standardised. We do so for a number of reasons. First, we believe that rationalisation can be achieved with a minimum of disruption and would foster a greater regional identity. Second, diocesan representation in the national institutions can then draw on these established groupings. We want to see the dioceses properly represented in the workings of the Council. Third, whilst we believe that regional offices would add an unnecessary tier of administration, the standardisation of regional groupings might be a prelude to the regionalisation of certain specific functions, which might in due course be carried out by one diocese on behalf of the whole region.

10.14 We have looked into and analysed the composition of the regional groupings as they stand at present. Our provisional conclusion is that the following arrangement of dioceses would result in the fewest changes overall for the individuals involved. We recommend that the six groupings set out in the table below should become the basis of all regional groupings in the future. It is likely that bishops in the North East, Midlands and South East groupings might wish to sub-divide these groups, as at present, making nine groupings. The archdeacons of the

Northern Province might wish to continue to meet as one group, and the South East grouping to remain sub-divided. We believe these minor variations are compatible with a basic desire for standardisation. The new groupings would also be very similar to the nine Government Standard Economic Regions, which we understand would be an advantage. We accept that the new groupings would involve Southwell remaining separate from the remainder of the Northern Province.

## Proposed standardised regional groupings

**North West**

Blackburn
Carlisle
Chester
Liverpool
Manchester
Sodor & Man

**North East**

| | |
|---|---|
| Bradford | (N) |
| Durham | (NE) |
| Newcastle | (NE) |
| Ripon | (N) |
| Sheffield | (N) |
| Wakefield | (N) |
| York | (NE) |

**Midlands**

| | |
|---|---|
| Birmingham | (WM) |
| Coventry | (WM) |
| Derby | (EM) |
| Hereford | (WM) |
| Leicester | (EM) |
| Lichfield | (EM) |
| Lincoln | (EM) |
| Southwell | (EM) |
| Worcester | (WM) |

**East Anglia**

Chelmsford
Ely
Norwich
Peterborough
St Albans
St Edmundsbury & Ipswich

**South West**

Bath & Wells
Bristol
Exeter
Gloucester
Salisbury
Truro

**South East**

| | |
|---|---|
| Canterbury | (SE) |
| Chichester | (S) |
| Europe | (SE) |
| Guildford | (SE) |
| London | (SE) |
| Oxford | (S) |
| Portsmouth | (S) |
| Rochester | (SE) |
| Southwark | (SE) |
| Winchester | (S) |

**Key to possible sub-divisions of groupings:** N = Northern; NE = North East; WM = West Midlands; EM = East Midlands; SE = South East; S = South.

## Other issues

10.15 The Church Commissioners set in train in mid-1994 a rolling programme of reviews of their activities, paying particular regard to their cost-effectiveness and taking full account of the views of dioceses. By early 1995 three of the working groups had reported and the Commission welcomes the resulting internal savings and those which will flow when certain functions, particularly in the areas of housing and pastoral reorganisation, are transferred to dioceses or cease altogether. Once those changes requiring legislation have been implemented, considerable savings at the centre will result with little or no extra cost to dioceses. We hope this review process will continue and that the Council will be vigilant in ensuring that all costs and activities are scrutinised and carefully controlled. There will, however, be certain costs transferred to dioceses under our recommendations which we identify and explain in the next chapter (paragraphs 11.3 and 11.4).

10.16 There are a number of substantive issues which neither our timescale nor our terms of reference have allowed us to examine in detail. The Pastoral Measure (revised in 1983) sets out procedures relating to pastoral reorganisation, redundant churches and numerous other matters. We hope that the Council would be able to undertake a fundamental review of the Measure in due course and consider particularly if the appeals procedures for pastoral schemes might be simplified. We are also concerned that, under the current legislative framework, the Dioceses Commission is unable to take any strategic view on matters of diocesan reorganisation such as the alteration of diocesan boundaries or the creation or abolition of diocesan or suffragan sees. Moreover, the establishment of archdeaconries is considered by the Church Commissioners and the establishment of suffragan bishoprics by the Dioceses Commission, despite the fact that both are interrelated aspects of diocesan organisation. As was noted in chapter 3, neither the Dioceses Commission nor the Church Commissioners has any power to initiate proposals under the Dioceses Measure or the Pastoral Measure; proposals can only be considered when put forward by a diocesan bishop. We recommend that the Council should at an early stage review these issues with a view to encouraging more proactive and strategic consideration of these aspects of the organisation of the Church.

## The deanery

10.17 A report on the organisation of the Church of England would be incomplete without reference to the deanery and the deanery synod. We

106

are conscious that the deanery often provides an appropriate unit for local clergy and lay people to join in worship, fellowship and discussion. On the other hand, it is sometimes suggested that the deanery is an unnecessary level in the Church's organisation and that it needs a new identity and purpose if it is to continue. There are very real issues here which we have not tackled because they do not fall within our terms of reference. The Review of Synodical Government is, however, examining the role of the deanery synod.

# 11

# Financial matters

## Central costs

11.1  The Church Commissioners at present pay for their own administrative costs and those of the Church of England Pensions Board and either contribute towards, or pay the whole of, the administrative costs of a number of other Church bodies. These amounted in 1994 to £7.6 million (excluding asset management costs). The cost of the General Synod and its Boards and Councils (£6.5 million) is apportioned on dioceses. Over half of the administrative costs of the national activities of the Church of England are therefore funded by the Commissioners and the remainder by the dioceses. The total costs of the national functions (including the cost of training for the ministry) amount to 3% of the total cost of the Church of England (which is at least £615 million a year).

11.2  The Church Commissioners have increasingly been asked to pay for the administrative costs of many activities not directly related to their asset management functions. Every pound used to finance central costs results in one pound less being available for selective allocation to the needier dioceses. In the changing financial climate that now prevails, we believe it should be for the Church as a whole to decide which organisations and activities should be funded nationally. The best way to secure this is for as much as possible of this cost to be funded by the dioceses through the budget for national Church responsibilities. The Church should be able to decide, in the context of its overall priorities, what elements of central expenditure should be met from the income from the historic assets (which would otherwise be available for allocation to the dioceses) and what should be met from apportionment on the dioceses nationally. We hope that improved communications and consultation, coupled with the transfer of responsibility for funding these activities to dioceses, will serve to facilitate the consideration of these issues.

11.3  The administrative costs and support provided by the Church Commissioners to other bodies should be confined to costs associated with the management of their assets. Support for diocesan bishops and cathedrals (including the cost of Lambeth Palace Library) is part of the Commissioners' historic obligations, and by analogy those assets should also support the secretariat of the House of Bishops. These should continue to be met from their income but all decisions on the level of this expenditure would in future pass to the Council. The clergy payroll is administered centrally as a service to dioceses and the costs of administering it should be billed by the Council to dioceses. It should be a matter for the dioceses to decide, on the grounds of cost-effectiveness, if they wish the centralised arrangement to continue. However, a piecemeal solution with some using the centre and some their own payrolls would not be efficient. The costs associated with the management of any assets transferred for pensions would form part of diocesan contributions to the pensions fund. It is our view that all other administrative costs and grants should be met by the dioceses through the budget for national Church responsibilities. Moreover, funding should be transparent. For example, we look to bishops and others to charge their expenses while engaged in Council business not to their own general expenses account but to the budget of the Council or the relevant committee. In this way, it would be possible to see the true cost of each activity.

11.4 The overall effect of the changes proposed in paragraph 11.3 is illustrated in the following table (using 1994 figures):

|  | Amount met by Church Commissioners | Amount apportioned to Dioceses | To be charged directly to the dioceses |
|---|---|---|---|
| AT PRESENT | £m | £m | £m |
| Pensions Board – administration (a) | 2.1 | – | – |
| Support for other bodies | 0.8 | – | – |
| Suffragan bishops' costs (inc. £0.1m admin.) | 2.8 | – | – |
| Clergy payroll administration | 0.3 | – | – |
| Commissioners' asset management (b) | 5.4 | – | – |
| National Church functions (CCs) | 4.3 | – | – |
| National Church responsibilities (CBF) | – | 6.6 | – |
| Training | – | 6.6 | – |
|  | 15.7 | 13.2 | – |
| PROPOSED |  |  |  |
| Pensions Board – administration | – | 2.1(c) | – |
| Support for other bodies | – | 0.8 | – |
| Suffragan bishops' costs | – | – | 2.8 |
| Clergy payroll administration | – | – | 0.3 |
| Commissioners' asset management | 5.4 (c) | – | – |
| National Church responsibilities | 0.8 | 10.1 | – |
| Training | – | 6.6 | – |
|  | 6.2 | 19.6 | 3.1 |

(a)   Includes cost of pensions payroll administration and other services provided by the Commissioners to the Pensions Board.

(b)   The investment management costs of the Pensions Board and the CBF have been ignored in this table.

(c)   Part of these costs will in future fall on the pension fund.

It will be apparent that, other things being equal, the apportionment on dioceses would rise (at current prices) from £13.2 million to up to £19.6 million. On the other hand the total of central costs met from the Church Commissioners' income would reduce substantially. Two important consequences flow from this change. First, subject to decisions about the total amount of income which they are able to distribute, there would be a significant increase in the resources available from the Church Commissioners (through the Council) for selective allocation to the needier dioceses. Second, the proportion of central costs included in the annual budget coming before the General Synod for approval would be much higher than at present, thus increasing the element of synodical accountability. We believe that this transfer of funding responsibility (which does not involve any net increase in total costs at the centre) is an important way of ensuring that the Church is able to respond more flexibly to the requirements of those areas of greatest need by releasing a greater proportion of the Commissioners' funds for discretionary allocation. Precisely how this mechanism would work in practice would need to be the subject of early discussion between dioceses and the national Church bodies, to ensure that the total effects of the changes were fully quantified and understood and that they were introduced in a way which was acceptable to the dioceses. By bringing a larger area of central expenditure within the purview of the Council and the General Synod budget, we hope that the Church would feel a greater sense of responsibility for its national functions and for ordering priorities in the allocation of scarce resources.

11.5 An important proviso in the previous paragraph is contained in the words 'other things being equal'. In practice other things would not be equal. Leaving aside factors such as inflation, which would affect costs generally, we are proposing a new structure for the Church's national organisations whose primary objective is to increase their effectiveness. The changes proposed would not commend themselves to the Church if this new structure was likely to cost more than the present one. Indeed, we think it essential that significant savings should be seen to be within our grasp. Nevertheless it is a matter of great difficulty at this stage to measure the savings which may be achievable. Some of the issues are outlined in the next two paragraphs.

11.6 There are significant differences between the conditions of service of staff employed by the different Church organisations. For example, variations exist in pay arrangements, pension schemes and concessionary mortgage benefits. It would clearly be necessary to standardise these as soon as possible, whilst ensuring that existing staff were treated fairly.

Civil Service pay arrangements at present apply to staff in all of the central Church structures. Major changes are being made to the Civil Service itself and its pay arrangements are becoming increasingly fragmented, but it is not yet clear what effect the possible disappearance of an appropriate Civil Service reference point might have on the overall salary bill. We are also keen that grading structures should wherever possible be sufficiently flexible to improve working patterns and the motivation and development of staff. For these reasons, any eventual savings may turn out to be less than or greater than might otherwise be expected. The staff who at present serve the central organisations of the Church must not be unfairly disadvantaged by the changes we propose. We must harness their energies to secure the implementation of these new arrangements.

11.7 The Council represents an entirely new way of co-ordinating the national business of the Church. It would be contrary to our underlying objectives if the new staffing structure were to be based merely on bringing the existing organisations together and looking for efficiency savings. A much more dynamic approach is needed. In particular, the rigid and complex committee structure which has for so many years dominated the way in which many Church House staff work must be radically altered in the early years of the new Council's life. There are over a hundred committees currently serviced by Church House staff. There must be a rigorous rolling programme of assessment of the need for all the committees; it is not, however, possible to say at this stage what might be the staff (and therefore cost) implications of the replacement of much of the Board and committee structure. We would expect the Council in its early years also to consider the support given to other Church bodies, such as the Church Urban Fund, alongside other national Church responsibilities. Modest savings on building services and office services should result from a single location for all staff at the centre as envisaged in paragraph 5.47. Further savings might be found if part of the Church's administrative staff were relocated out of London, but we see this as a longer term issue, and the prime objective must be for the great majority of the staff to be located in the same building to facilitate the process of working as one body.

11.8 Despite the difficulties, we have carefully examined the likely staffing and other requirements of the proposed arrangements. Clearly, until the Council is formed and has worked out its plans in detail, it is impossible to be precise about its costs. In the short run, say for the first two or three years, it would be unwise to expect worthwhile savings to be achieved. Indeed, the process of transition is likely to have an adverse impact during this period (for which some provision is being made through the CBF budget for 1996/7). Looking beyond this initial stage, some broad calculations we have made, based on what we believe to be reasonable assumptions, lead us to expect that savings of between £0.75 million and £1 million *per annum* should be achievable; furthermore the Council should consider setting this as a target. We think it unrealistic to be more precise at this juncture.

11.9 We fully recognise that considerable efforts have been made in recent years to reduce the administrative costs at the centre; in particular, the number of staff at the Church Commissioners has reduced from 400 to 270 since 1980. We welcome these achievements and encourage this continued drive for realistic economies. The CBF Budget Reviews are on target to reduce staff costs and grants to other bodies by 10% between 1995 and 1997. The Church Commissioners' Activity Based Reviews are already yielding substantial savings which are expected to rise to about £800,000 a year once all the necessary changes – including through legislation in some areas of work – have been implemented. We have looked at these reviews in some detail. They are sound and thorough. We hope that the review process will be maintained and will include the Pensions Board's functions.

11.10 The Commission has not found immediate scope for further drastic reductions in the costs of the centre. That was not our task, nor would we have considered it right for us to hunt mercilessly for savings in each area of work. Our recommendations take account of the financial issues but are not finance-led. Instead, we have sought to identify the most appropriate level within the Church's organisation for aspects of the Church's mission and ministry, and then to ensure that all those functions which belong at the national level are carried out not only efficiently and effectively, but also economically. The Council would provide the machinery for securing this. We have also set out more clearly than has hitherto been done what should (and consequently what should not) be financed from the Church Commissioners' income. We are confident that the changes at the national level which we recommend would lead both to an improved level of service and, beyond the transitional period, to an appreciable reduction in cost.

## Flows of money

11.11 The funding of activities within the Church of England is complex. We have therefore attempted to set out the major items of cost and the sources of finance: where necessary we have used estimates. The figures should be seen as very approximate and are for illustration only.

|  | £m (1993) |
| --- | --- |
| **Costs** | |
| Stipends and housing | 205 |
| Pensions | 79 |
| Worship and buildings | 250 |
| Community and charities | 37 |
| Training | 7 |
| National Church responsibilities | 7 |
| Administration (mainly dioceses and parishes) | 30 |
|  | £615 million |
| **Financed by** | |
| Parishes | |
| Covenanted giving (including tax recovered) | 157 |
| Other giving | 134 |
| Other income | 89 |
| Church Commissioners | 153 |
| Pensions Board | 10 |
| Cathedral and diocesan endowments | 64 |
| From reserves | 8 |
|  | £615 million |

11.12 Until the early to middle years of this century the assumption was that the parson would find his material support (living) from the various endowments of his office (benefice) and the right to receive taxes (tithes). Redistribution and the addition of fresh endowment from time to time, augmentation from increased giving from parishes, clergymen with private incomes, and the acceptance by very many others of clerical poverty, kept this traditional financial picture alive for longer than might have been expected. But the relentless inroads of inflation and increasing inequalities between clergy stipends had all but destroyed it by the end of the 1950s, in practice if not in folk memory. Fortunately, considerable progress has been made towards the harmonisation of stipends nationally. For administrative convenience almost all clergy are now paid through a central payroll.

11.13 Stipends and other costs associated with the mission and ministry of the Church at parish, diocesan and national levels are met in part
from assets owned by the Church Commissioners and dioceses, which
constitute the Church's inherited wealth. However, the income from
these sources provides less than 30% of the estimated £615 million a
year which it costs to run the Church of England. Now, substantial
though the inherited endowments still are, it is the voluntary giving of
the laity in the parishes, channelled through diocesan quotas, which
increasingly provides the material support of the ministry, with the
income available for allocation from historic endowments being channelled increasingly towards areas of need. These financial realities in
their turn are reshaping our structures. They have reinforced awareness
of the importance and power of both the (gathered) congregation as a
growing source of money and of the diocesan board of finance as, in
effect, the (voluntary taxation) mechanism through which that money is
asked for and raised in sufficient quantity.

11.14 We recognise that as the Church of England's dependence on
inherited wealth reduces, parishes and dioceses are faced with a hard
challenge and painful decisions lie ahead for all of us. Nevertheless, we
do welcome the increased reliance on voluntary and sacrificial giving.
A living Church should depend primarily on living members for its sur-
vival and growth. Those who are giving should be able to see how their
money is being spent and have the opportunity, directly or indirectly,
to influence those decisions. This expectation plays a healthy part in
ensuring that scarce resources are used efficiently and effectively. Our
proposals seek to enhance the accountability of those taking policy and
resource decisions, whilst stressing that those directly charged with the
responsibility for taking decisions should have the trust of the Church
as a whole. When decisions have been properly reached there is an
obligation on us to accept them so that we can work as one body.

11.15 We do not believe it is appropriate for the stipends of individual
clergy to be set by the members of their parochial church councils. Each
parish is part of a national Church which has a responsibility to ensure
that all its stipendiary clergy are paid at a fair level. That level is set by
the Central Stipends Authority, which is a partnership involving the dioceses and the centre and whose functions would be exercised by the new
Council. It exists to encourage uniformity of stipend levels, both in the
interest of equity and (for the benefit of the Church as a whole) to
encourage clergy mobility. It would not be efficient or appropriate for
each parish to run a payroll, from which their clergy would be paid.
Fewer than twenty staff administer the central payroll, payment of tax

and many other matters relating to the payment of 17,600 serving and retired clergy. Cost effectiveness requires that the clergy payroll function should currently be located at national, rather than diocesan, level although the dioceses should review from time to time whether they wish to assume this function themselves. A central payroll operation brings benefits from economies of scale but it does mean that those who provide the resources with which the clergy are paid each month have to route the resources to the central operation. It is a sound principle that monies for stipends and, especially, for pensions should be pooled and held at one remove from the parish.

11.16 We believe that money flows within the Church must be rationalised and better explained. This can be achieved at two levels. First, parishioners are entitled to know what they are paying for. We hope that all dioceses will soon be able to provide parishes with a statement of what their vicar and any other stipendiary clergy cost, which will include their housing, stipend, employer's National Insurance, pension and training. Clergy expenses (which should be met in full by the parish) together with a share of diocesan overheads and of the cost of the national Church must be added to this to show the total cost of ministry in that parish. Guidelines and standard definitions for calculating the total cost of ministry should be set nationally to reduce variations between dioceses. The finance committee which we describe in appendix C might be asked to provide these. The parish may be requested to provide more or less than this amount depending on the respective needs and resources of the parish and diocese. Such decisions do not belong at the national level and it would not be appropriate for us to comment on the amount which a parish should be asked to provide, but we do believe that parishes are entitled to know whether they are being supported by or whether they are supporting other parishes.

11.17 We put forward three principles:

- parishes should be provided by dioceses with a statement of the cost of ministry in their parish, to include a proportionate contribution to activities funded at a diocesan and national level

- parochial, diocesan and national activities should all be seen as supportive of each other; those engaged in policy-making at each level should communicate more effectively how money is spent to those who are contributing

- there needs to be an acceptance of giving to, and being supported by, others; trusting others to make decisions is inherent in the image of the Church as the body of Christ but that trust should be reciprocated by open, fair and understandable means of discerning need and of reallocating resources.

11.18 Second, we turn to the flow of money between dioceses and the centre. The law has required that a number of accounts and trust funds are held nationally. The need for many transactions could be saved if many or all of these accounts were held by dioceses. The Church Commissioners have already come to the view, which we welcome, that diocesan pastoral accounts and diocesan stipends fund capital accounts should pass to dioceses. We recommend that all relevant trust monies should be held by dioceses. After the appropriate legislation has been passed, dioceses would be free to invest funds locally or, if they wished, through the Church Commissioners' Property Pool or the investment funds offered by CCLA Investment Management Limited or whatever central investment vehicles may from time to time be made available to Church bodies.

11.19 We referred in paragraph 11.13 to the two main sources of the Church's income. There are, we believe, further sources which are worthy of serious consideration. Fundraising has traditionally been confined largely to local appeals to repair church buildings, yet the Church Urban Fund and other charities have demonstrated clearly that there is a considerable willingness by individuals, trusts and companies to support clearly focused good causes with which they can identify and which contribute to areas of need. We believe that individuals and organisations, both within and outside the Church, would be ready to fund certain 'mission' projects in which people are actively involved in Christian programmes, but where the local church is unable to meet the full cost. Many charities also rely heavily on income from legacies; we firmly believe that many more people could and should be encouraged to leave money to the Church of which they are part and which has sustained them in life. We therefore welcome the CBF's development of a legacies strategy. All of these possibilities require careful examination and the Church should not be afraid to take professional advice, much of which is available within the Church, to assist in releasing these potential sources of giving for the work of the Church. The specific tasks of the Council will include not only the effective stewardship of central resources but taking active steps to enhance them. We recommend that fundraising and promoting legacies should be on the agenda of the Council's finance committee.

# 12

# Summary of conclusions
# and principal recommendations

## The Commission's approach

12.1   The Archbishops' Commission has reviewed the machinery for central policy and resource direction in the Church of England. There is at present no single focus for the exercise of those functions. Responsibility for them is dispersed between the Archbishops of Canterbury and York, the House of Bishops, the General Synod and its Boards and Councils, the Central Board of Finance, the Church Commissioners and the Church of England Pensions Board.

12.2   We make recommendations, which would require legislation by Measure, for improving the effectiveness of the machinery for central policy and resource direction in supporting the ministry and mission of the Church to the nation as a whole. We have taken an interest in the culture of the central institutions as well as in their structures.

12.3   We urge that our major recommendations be taken as a package of interrelated reforms. We do not believe the necessary changes would be achieved if only some of our recommendations were implemented. Our key proposals are intended to trigger a process of reform which the new central structures should pursue with vigour. The centre must in future be more adaptable and have an executive which can respond flexibly to changing circumstances. In seeking the right balance for the future, we have sought guidance from theology and in prayer.

12.4   In the light of the biblical teaching that the Church is the body of Christ, we must all work together as one body. The basic structure of the Church as it already exists is, we believe, capable of offering an exemplary way of working together. Our proposals build on the Anglican tradition which combines leadership by bishops with governance by synods. They draw on the conviction that God in his goodness has already given to the Church the resources it needs to do his work.

12.5   Most of the work of the Church of England is carried out in the dioceses and the parishes. The Church does not have and does not need an omnicompetent centre. There are, however, functions which can only be, and have to be, carried out by the Church as a whole and our recommendations focus on how those are handled.

12.6 We believe our recommendations leave undisturbed the traditional relationship between Church and State in England.

12.7 We have identified in our report some real and perceived shortcomings of the existing central structures of the Church. They can be broadly summarised as follows:

- people are dissatisfied with and lack confidence in the national performance of the Church especially, in recent years, the Church Commissioners

- there is no single body with overall responsibility for co-ordinating those aspects of Church policy which are necessarily the subject of central planning, especially in relation to the allocation of resources

- there is a cat's cradle of autonomous and semi-autonomous bodies with distinctive, but sometimes overlapping, functions which are a source of confusion and wasteful duplication of effort

- much of the work of the national bodies is committee-bound

- there is no national equivalent to the coherence achieved in the dioceses through the workings of the model of the Bishop-in-Synod.

Recent events have illustrated the seriousness of these defects, which are the outcome of a long history of piecemeal development. We are now presented with an opportunity to seek a remedy for them.

## Recommendations

12.8 We propose a reform of the national institutions of the Church which builds on the model of the Bishop-in-Synod. The Church should have a new **National Council** to provide a focus for leadership and executive responsibility. The Archbishop of Canterbury would chair it and the Archbishop of York would be its vice-chairman.

12.9 The Council would act as an executive serving the Church. It would help the Church to work as one body, taking an overview of all the policy and resource issues which properly require resolution at the national level. The Council would analyse the issues and take responsibility for proposing strategies for dealing with them. This emphasis on shouldering practical responsibility and being accountable for it is new:

the buck would stop with the Council and it would be answerable for its work. It would balance consultation with leadership.

12.10   At the same time the Council should take care to respect the roles of the parishes and the dioceses. The Council would carry out much of its work in direct contact with the dioceses, and should seek to restore the confidence of the dioceses and the parishes in the work of the Church at the national level, much of which is performed in support of them. No function should be performed at the centre which can more effectively or more appropriately be carried out at the diocesan level.

12.11   Policy and resource issues should be grouped into four areas of activity: resources for ministry (human resources); mission resources; financial resources; and heritage and legal services. The Council should include four part-time executive chairmen, chosen for their skills, to exercise responsibility for leadership in each of these areas. The membership of the Council should also include two members elected by the House of Bishops, the elected clergy and lay leaders of the General Synod and the Chairman of its Business Committee, and the Council's chief executive and head of staff, a new post of Secretary General. The Archbishops would be able to nominate an additional three members chosen for their skill and experience. They, and the four executive chairmen, would be nominated by the Archbishops and their appointments would be approved by the General Synod.

12.12   The House of Bishops would exercise its leadership by developing with the assistance of the Council a vision for the broad direction of the Church, offering it for debate in the General Synod and the Church as a whole. This vision would in turn influence the work of the Council, which would seek the guidance of the House of Bishops on its overall plan and strategy and then present them to the General Synod for endorsement.

12.13   The Council would prepare the budget for national Church responsibilities and present it to the General Synod for approval, setting it within the wider context of an overview of the Church's finances as a whole. The Church Commissioners would be radically slimmed down but remain as managers and trustees of the central historic assets of the Church. Almost all their other functions, including decisions about the allocation of their income, would be transferred to the Council.

12.14   We are confident our proposals would enable the Church to develop a coherent and strategic view on the issues it faces, especially on financial matters and, under the leadership of the Council, to find strategies for dealing with them.

12.15 The functions of the National Council would include:

- helping the Church to develop a clearer sense of direction, of the opportunities presented to it, and of its needs and priorities if it is better to fulfil its mission in the world, drawing on the guidance of the House of Bishops, and offering the result for the approval of the General Synod

- ensuring that policies and strategies are developed to meet those needs and priorities, and to exploit the opportunities given it by God

- overseeing the direction of Church staff and other resources at the national level in support of the agreed policies

- supporting the dioceses and helping them in their work, including co-ordinating their activities where they agree this is desirable in order to help them better to achieve the Church's overall mission.

12.16 The tasks of the National Council would include:

- assessment of the overall financial and human resource needs of the Church, and planning ahead accordingly, including not only the effective stewardship of these resources but taking active steps to enhance them

- determination, within a framework agreed by the House of Bishops and the General Synod and after discussion with the dioceses, of the allocation of income from the Church Commissioners' assets

- management, in discussion with the dioceses, of arrangements for redistributing resources within the Church to help even up the financial position of dioceses and respond to the needs of mission, and the proposed apportionment of national costs among the dioceses

- approval for submission to the General Synod of the budgets for training for the ministry and national Church responsibilities

- presentation to the General Synod or the House of Bishops, as appropriate, of legislative or other proposals designed to help the Church respond to its needs and priorities and to enhance the effectiveness of the Church's ministry and mission

- oversight as necessary of the work of the various committees or Boards of the Council and of its staff.

12.17 The Council collectively, and its members individually, would have a public responsibility to enhance the leadership and coherence of the Church. We recommend a change in the style in which work is done at the centre with results, not paper, as the desired outcome. There are over a hundred committees currently serviced by Church House staff. The Church must move away from this culture. We therefore strongly urge that the Council's committee structure should be kept as small as possible and that in due course the national Board and Council structure (which would come under the authority of the Council) should be reviewed and the number of committees involved substantially cut down. The purpose and achievement of every committee and group should in future be subject to regular scrutiny. As few standing bodies as possible should be established. More work should be done in small groups with a specific focus and a limited life. Because we believe the Council must be free to organise its work as efficiently and effectively as from time to time it judges possible we do not prescribe a comprehensive committee structure for it.

12.18 The staff of the Archbishops, the Central Board of Finance (including the General Synod Office and the Synod's Boards and Councils), the Church Commissioners and the Church of England Pensions Board should merge to form a single central staff service, pooling their expertise and helping the Church to work as one body. As many as possible of the Church's central staff (other than the Archbishops' personal staff) should be based in one building, probably at Church House, Westminster, to further this cohesion. The Church should make more effective use of the skills of its staff, trusting them and giving them flexibility to get on with agreed tasks as they think best, and holding them to account for the result.

12.19 The structure we propose would provide the **Archbishops** with the institutional framework they need to enable them to provide effective leadership. We believe the time already spent by the Archbishops in the existing separate bodies, in formal and informal meetings to hold the ring between them and weigh up their separate representations, would be more effectively spent in leading the new Council and conferring between meetings with its members and staff. The Archbishops would continue to select and appoint their own personal staff, who would become members of the national office staff.

12.20 The **House of Bishops** should in future play a more sharply focused and purposeful role. We recommend that the House of Bishops should at regular intervals develop and articulate a vision for the direction of the Church of England. This would be debated by the General Synod and the Council would be responsible for the strategies and resources for translating the vision into action. We doubt if the House of Bishops could develop its role in this way under the present arrangements. We recommend that it undertakes a radical review of its priorities, agenda and resourcing. The Council should provide a proper level of staff support for the work of the House of Bishops. The Council would also account to the House for those aspects of the work of the national office (such as selection and training for the ordained ministry) which fell specifically within the House's responsibility.

12.21 The proposed National Council would have a close relationship with the **General Synod**. The membership of the Council would include the Archbishops and seven persons directly elected by the Synod or its Houses and the others would be nominated by the Archbishops and have their appointments approved by the Synod. All members of the Council would become members of the Synod. The Council would take over the functions of the General Synod's Standing Committee and its Policy Committee, the Advisory Board of Ministry and the Central Board of Finance, all of which would cease to exist. The other Boards and Councils would come under the authority of the Council.

12.22 There would be an important measure of public accountability of the Council to the Synod which as a representative assembly must be able to question, to seek and obtain information, and to express opinions which would influence the formation of policy. If, as we propose, some of the central administration costs which are now borne by the Church Commissioners instead become part of the budget for national Church responsibilities (so that the equivalent amount can be released for selective allocation), a larger proportion of central costs would come under the scrutiny of the General Synod. The staff of the **Central Board of Finance** would become members of the single national office under the Council.

12.23 The **Church of England Pensions Board** should be reconstituted (see paragraph 9.11) to act as trustees of the pensions schemes (and in due course of the new clergy pensions fund). The responsibility for administering pensions and for proposing pensions policy would rest with the Council. The staff of the Pensions Board would become staff of the national office.

12.24 Our recommendations would involve substantial changes for the **Church Commissioners for England**. They would continue to embody the historic partnership between Church and State as managers and trustees of the historic central assets of the Church. However, the Council would take over responsibility for all their other functions, including decisions about the allocation of the income which the

Commissioners can make available for distribution. We recommend that, subject to discussion with Ministers and the approval of Parliament, the composition of the Commissioners should be radically changed, reducing the total number from 95 to 15. The staff of the Church Commissioners would become staff of the national office.

12.25 The amount of income which the Commissioners are currently making available is probably more than can be sustained in the future if the real value of their assets is to be maintained. Much of the income is already committed to the payment of pensions. This support is of great value to the dioceses and parishes and is paid to them regardless of their own resources. It will become increasingly important for the Council to make the best use of the remaining amounts which can be made available for selective allocation to the areas of greatest need. The Commissioners currently pay for their own administration costs and contribute towards the administration costs of other central Church bodies. In order to increase the amount available for selective allocation, and to introduce greater transparency in the costs of the centre, we recommend that in future the majority of those costs should (like the rest of the budget for national Church responsibilities) be shared among the dioceses through apportionment, which takes account of the inequalities in the dioceses' resources.

12.26 In working with the dioceses, the Council should develop an improved dialogue and an open sharing of information. It should have members of diocesan boards of finance on its finance committee.

12.27 The dioceses have no formal role in briefing their representatives on the General Synod and it is clear that they do not feel that diocesan concerns on issues of policy and resources are effectively conveyed. The dioceses should look at how they brief their diocesan representatives on the financial and other implications for the dioceses of the General Synod's work.

12.28 In our report we affirm the value of the work done at parish, deanery and diocesan level, and by those who hold positions of leadership in the national institutions of the Church and those who serve them. In addition to the principal recommendations outlined in this chapter we also make other detailed recommendations, including the following areas:

- a new partnership of mutual recognition and responsibility between dioceses, parishes and the Church at national level (paragraph 5.2)

- improved communications between parishes, dioceses and the national level (paragraphs 10.7 and 10.8)

- the support of bishops (paragraphs 8.24 to 8.33) and cathedrals (paragraphs 8.34 to 8.36)

- a joint advisory group on ethical investment (paragraph 5.40)

- a new post of Clerk of the General Synod (paragraph 6.38)

- working relationships between the Council and the Church Commissioners (paragraph 8.18 and 8.19)

- standardised regional groupings for meetings of bishops, archdeacons and diocesan office holders (paragraphs 7.8, 10.13 and 10.14).

Our proposals for change at the national level do have financial implications (see paragraphs 11.1 to 11.10), but in aggregate we do not expect them to cost more.

12.29 We are unanimous in making these proposals for reform. We are confident that they would enable the central institutions of the Church to be more effective and efficient in making policy and in directing resources. We hope they will be implemented swiftly so that the Church can more effectively work as one body in the service of God and his world.

# Appendix A

# Terms of reference, membership and background to the Commission's work

## Terms of reference

A.1    'To review the machinery for central policy and resource direction in the Church of England, and to make recommendations for improving its effectiveness in supporting the ministry and mission of the Church to the nation as a whole.'

## Membership

A.2    Chairman:    The Rt Revd Michael Turnbull (Bishop of Durham)

Members:    The Rt Hon. the Lord Bridge of Harwich (Former Lord of Appeal in Ordinary and Former Chairman of the Ecclesiastical Committee of Parliament; also Chairman of the Review of Synodical Government)

Sir Michael Colman Bt (First Church Estates Commissioner; Chairman, Reckitt and Colman plc)

Sir Brian Cubbon GCB (Former Permanent Under Secretary of State at the Northern Ireland Office and Home Office)

The Very Revd Dr David Edwards OBE (Provost Emeritus of Southwark)

Mr Howard Gracey (Chairman, Church of England Pensions Board; Former Senior Partner, R Watson and Sons)

Miss Sylvia Green (Diocesan Secretary, Hereford)

Mr John Jordan (Consultant, KPMG; Former Head of Operations and Financial Management, KPMG Consulting)

The Ven. Stephen Lowe (Archdeacon of Sheffield)

Professor David McClean CBE QC (Chairman of the General Synod's House of Laity; Pro-Vice Chancellor and Professor of Law, Sheffield University)

Mr Alan McLintock (Chairman, Central Board of Finance; Chairman, Allchurches Trust; President (Former Chairman), Woolwich Building Society; Former Chairman, Ecclesiastical Insurance Group)

Mr Humphrey Norrington (Former Vice-Chairman, Barclays Bank)

Mr Bryan Sandford (Chairman, York Diocesan Board of Finance)

| | |
|---|---|
| Theological Consultant: | The Rt Revd Stephen Sykes (Bishop of Ely) |
| Assessors: | Mr Patrick Locke (Secretary to the Church Commissioners) |
| | Mr Philip Mawer (Secretary-General of the General Synod) |
| | Dr Andrew Purkis (Archbishop of Canterbury's Secretary for Public Affairs) |
| Secretary: | Ms Janet Lewis-Jones |
| Assistant Secretary: | Mr Mark Humphriss |
| Personal Secretary: | Mrs Ronnie Ferguson |

127

## Number of meetings

A.3    The Commission met on 15 occasions between March 1994 and July 1995. Residential meetings were held at Aylesford Priory, Kent (15 and 16 April 1994) and at the Whirlow Grange Conference Centre, Sheffield (13 and 14 November 1994 and 9 to 11 March 1995). The other meetings were held at Lambeth Palace, on each occasion for the greater part of a day. The Archbishop and Mrs Carey were not only generous with their hospitality for those meetings but were also kind enough to provide accommodation for the Commission Office through-out the course of its work. We are most grateful to them.

## Finance

A.4    The Central Board of Finance made a financial contribution towards the work of the Commission of £40,000 (£5,000 of which was given by the Corporation of the Church House) and the Church Commissioners gave £60,000 and each body seconded a member of staff to assist the Secretary. Any additional expenses of the Commission were met by the Archbishops.

## Background

A.5    In the summer of 1992 the Church Commissioners' management of their resources was the subject of public criticism. In the light of that criticism, the Archbishop of Canterbury invited a small group chaired by the Bishop of Chelmsford to consider the alleged shortcomings and to make recommendations. The Lambeth Group (as it became known) reported in July 1993 and all the recommendations made have now been acted upon. One recommendation was

> The nature, the constitution and the management of Church affairs are very different from and more complex than most other organisations within which large scale assets and liabilities are managed and financial returns deployed. It would be appropriate for the Church to review its overall organisational structure in the light of its present-day activities and requirements. (III.1 and VIII.3)

After discussion and consultation with the bodies concerned, the Archbishops of Canterbury and York considered that such a review was desirable also on grounds wider than those considered by the Lambeth Group. They decided that it could best be undertaken by the formation of a Commission to examine the policy making and resource direction machinery of the Church of England and the terms of reference and membership of the Commission were announced on 16 February 1994. The Commission was asked to report to the Archbishops in the summer of 1995.

A.6    The Archbishops' Commission was asked to engage in the most wide-ranging overview of the national institutions of the Church that has ever been undertaken. We recognised the magnitude of this task, but also quickly realised that limitations had to be placed on what we could realistically achieve in little more than a year. In particular, we have been primarily concerned with organisational *structures* for policy making and resource direction at the national level, as our terms of reference required. We did not look at issues of substantive policy such as clergy conditions of service or the established nature of the Church. We hope that what we have said in this report will be of interest and relevance to all parts of the Church but we have not considered in any detail matters such as diocesan structures, the parish and deanery system, or the Church's legal system. That is not to say that we do not appreciate the value of their contribution to the life of the Church but simply that our own terms of reference were already wide enough.

## Other reviews

A.7    A number of other major reviews have either reported during the life of the Commission or are due to report in the next couple of years. The Commission has taken note of the Report of the Archbishops' Commission on Cathedrals. It is aware of, and warmly commends, the Consultative Paper issued in September 1994 by the Clergy Conditions of Service Steering Group, chaired by Sir Timothy Hoare. The Commission has been working in liaison with the Review of Synodical Government, under the chairmanship of Lord Bridge of Harwich. That Review's timescale has been extended to allow members of Lord Bridge's group to develop their recommendations in the light of our own. There are a number of other substantive issues currently facing the Church of England (and we refer particularly to pensions in our report). The Commission has been kept informed of this work and taken care to avoid overlap with it.

## Written evidence

A.8    We are very grateful to the 471 individuals and organisations who have written to the Commission, whether such contributions were unsolicited or in response to the invitations which appeared in *The Independent*, the *Church Times*, the *Church of England Newspaper* and a number of local and diocesan newspapers. Their submissions have made an important contribution to our work and we have reflected carefully on them. We take heart from the fact that our proposals are compatible with the majority of comments made to us both in writing and at consultations with the General Synod and other groups within the Church.

# Illustrative draft Measure

The draft clauses set out below are intended only to illustrate the kind of legislation that would be needed to give effect to the recommendations made in this report. They should not be regarded as complete or definitive at this stage. Legislation to implement any aspect of this report would have to be finalised following consultation and in the light of further research, and would have to reflect legislation in force at the time (e.g. on pensions). A full Measure would be accompanied by a memorandum explaining – as does the body of this report – the financial and other effects of the Measure.

## DRAFT CHURCH OF ENGLAND (CENTRAL INSTITUTIONS) MEASURE 199-

## ARRANGEMENT OF CLAUSES
## PART I

### National Council

1 Establishment of the National Council
2 Constitution
3 Chairmen
4 Functions
5 Accounts and audit
6 Annual report and accounts
7 Transfer of officers

# PART II

## Other institutions

# PART III

## General provisions

# SCHEDULES

## DRAFT OF A MEASURE PROPOSED TO BE PASSED BY THE GENERAL SYNOD OF THE CHURCH OF ENGLAND

To make better provision for the establishment and functions of the central institutions of the Church of England and for the management of the assets thereof.

# PART I

## National Council

Establishment of the National Council.

1   There shall be a body to be known as "the National Council of the Church of England", constituted in accordance with section 2 below, whose object shall be to co-ordinate, support and generally further the work and mission of the Church of England.

Constitution.

2   (1) The Council shall consist of:

(a) the Archbishops of Canterbury and York;

(b) the four executive chairmen appointed under section 3 below;

(c) the Prolocutors of the Convocations of Canterbury and York;

(d) the chairman and vice-chairman of the House of Laity;

(e) two bishops elected by the House of Bishops from among its members;

(f) the chairman of the Business Committee of the General Synod;

(g) such persons as may be appointed under subsection (2) below;

(h) the Secretary General.

(2) The General Synod, on the nomination of the Archbishops of Canterbury and York acting jointly, may appoint not more than three additional persons as members of the Council.

(3) The provisions of Schedule 1 to this Measure shall have effect with respect to the Council and its members, to the Council's proceedings and incidental powers and to the employment of staff and the service and conditions of their employment.

(4) The Council shall be an exempt charity for the purposes of the Charities Act 1993; and accordingly in Schedule 2 to that Act at the end there shall be inserted:

(zb) "the National Council of the Church of England."

1993 c. 10.

**Chairmen.**

3 (1) The Archbishop of Canterbury shall be the chairman of the Council and the Archbishop of York shall be the vice-chairman.

(2) There shall be four other chairmen of committees, to be known as executive chairmen, appointed by the General Synod on the nomination of the Archbishops of Canterbury and York acting jointly.

(3) Each of the executive chairmen shall act as such in connection with an area of activity of the Council to be determined by the Council.

4 (1) On the appointed day the functions of:

(a) the Standing Committee of the General Synod appointed in pursuance of paragraph 10(2) of Schedule 2 to the Synodical Government Measure 1969 except in so far as the Standing Orders of the General Synod otherwise provide;

(b) the Central Board of Finance; and

(c) the Church Commissioners other than the functions specified in section 9(1) below, shall be transferred to and become functions of the Council.

**Functions.**
**1969 No. 2.**

(2) Without prejudice to the generality of subsection (1) above it shall be the duty of the Council, as

from the appointed day, to consider and determine how to apply or distribute such sums as have been made available by the Church Commissioners under section 9(2) below.

(3) Any moneys made available by the Church Commissioners as aforesaid shall, if previously held by them subject to any trust or condition, be subject to the same trust or condition in the hands of the Council.

(4) Before determining the amount to be applied or distributed for the stipends and support of bishops the Council shall consult the Bishoprics Committee.

(5) As soon as practicable after the end of each year the Council shall cause a certificate to be issued to the Church Commissioners to the effect that the moneys made available by them have been applied or distributed in accordance with all relevant trusts and conditions.

Accounts and audit.

5 (1) The Council shall cause such accounts to be kept as may be required for the due performance and discharge of its functions.

(2) The accounts of the Council shall in every year be audited in such manner and by such person as the Council may direct, and the auditor's report thereon shall for the purposes of section 6 below be deemed to form part of the accounts.

(3) The Council shall appoint a committee consisting of three members of the Council whose duty it shall be to:

(a) examine the accounts of the Council; and

(b) consider and review all other aspects of the work of the Council.

Annual report and accounts.

6 As soon as practicable after the end of each year the Council shall prepare a report of its work and proceedings during that year, and shall cause the

134

report and accounts to be laid before the
General Synod.

Transfer of
officers.

7 On the appointed day every officer of the
Church Commissioners, the Central Board of
Finance and the Pensions Board shall be
transferred to and become an officer of the Council.

# PART II

# Other institutions

Church
Commissioners.

Geo. 6 No. 2.

8 (1) The Church Commissioners Measure
1947 shall be amended as follows.

(2) After section 5 there shall be inserted:

"Assets and
Audit
Committees.

5A. (1) There shall be two
committees, one to be known
as the Assets Committee and the
other as the Audit Committee,
which shall be constituted as follows:

(a) the Assets Committee shall
comprise:

(i) the First Church Estates
Commissioner;

(ii) two Commissioners elected by
them, being persons elected as
Commissioners in accordance
with paragraph 1(d), (e), (f) or
(g) of Schedule 1 to this
Measure; and

(iii) not less than three nor more
than five persons appointed for
three years by the Archbishop of
Canterbury, being persons who
in his opinion are well qualified
to assist in the management of
the assets of the Commissioners;

(b)  the Audit Committee shall comprise:

  (i)  two Commissioners elected by
       them, being persons elected as
       Commissioners as aforesaid; and
  (ii) three persons appointed for
       three years by the Archbishop of
       Canterbury;

(c)  the First Church Estates
     Commissioner shall be the chair-
     man of the Assets Committee and
     the Audit Committee shall elect one
     of its members to be its chairman.

(2) The functions of the Assets
Committee shall be as follows:

(a)  a duty to supervise and direct the
     arrangements made for the manage-
     ment of the assets of the
     Commissioners;

(b)  a duty to consider and report on
     any matter referred to it by the
     Commissioners.

(3) The functions of the Audit
Committee shall be as follows:

(a)  a duty to examine the accounts of
     the Commissioners;

(b)  a duty to consider and review all
     other aspects of the work of the
     Commissioners and the Assets
     Committee."

(3) In Schedule 1 for paragraph 1 there shall be
substituted:

"1. The Commissioners shall be:

(a)  the Archbishops of Canterbury and York;

(b)  the First and Second Church Estates
     Commissioners;

(c)  three persons appointed by Her Majesty;

136

(d) two bishops elected by the House of Bishops of the General Synod from among its members;

(e) a dean or provost elected by the deans and provosts who are members of the House of Clergy of the General Synod;

(f) two clerks in Holy Orders elected by the House of Clergy of the General Synod from among its members;

(g) three laymen elected by the House of Laity of the General Synod from among its members."

(4) The Board of Governors established by section 5 of that Measure and the General Purposes Committee established by section 6 thereof shall cease to exist. [Sections 5 and 6(1) to (4) of the 1947 Measure to be repealed]

Continuing functions of Church Commissioners.

9 (1) The Church Commissioners shall continue to have the following functions:

(a) a duty to act in all matters relating to the management of their assets, including power to sell, purchase, exchange and let land and make, realise and change investments;

1983 No. 1.

(b) the functions arising from section 77 of the Pastoral Measure 1983 in connection with diocesan pastoral accounts;

1 & 2 Eliz. 2 No. 2.

(c) the functions arising from section 2 of the Diocesan Stipends Funds Measure 1953 in connection with the capital and income accounts of diocesan stipends funds;

26 Geo. 5 & 1 Edw. 8 c.43.

(d) the functions arising from section 31(2) of the Tithe Act 1936 in connection with the repair of chancels of churches and other ecclesiastical buildings.

(2) It shall be the duty of the Church Commissioners in respect of each year, after consultation with the Council, to:

(a) determine and certify to the Council the amount of income from their assets which is to be made available to it; and

(b) pay that amount to the Council as and when requested by it.

Bishoprics Committee.

10 (1) There shall be a joint committee to be called the Bishoprics Committee, consisting of five persons appointed by the Council from among its members and five persons (including at least one lay person) appointed by the Church Commissioners from among their number.

(2) In making appointments to the Bishoprics Committee the Council and the Church Commissioners shall enter into consultation with a view to ensuring that the persons appointed include at least two diocesan bishops, two clerks in Holy Orders and two lay persons.

(3) It shall be the duty of the Bishoprics Committee to supervise and give general directions with regard to the administration by the officers of the Council of arrangements for paying the stipends of, and otherwise providing financial support for, bishops.

(4) The chairman of the Bishoprics Committee shall be appointed by the Archbishops of Canterbury and York acting jointly from among those of its members who are lay Church Commissioners.

Pensions Board
9 & 10 Eliz. 2
No. 3.

11 In section 21 of the Clergy Pensions Measure 1961 for subsection (3) there shall be substituted:

"(3) The Board shall consist of fifteen members appointed or elected as follows:

(a) the chairman shall be appointed by the Archbishops of Canterbury and York acting jointly;

(b) one bishop shall be elected by the House of Bishops of the General Synod;

(c) one lay officer of the Council shall be elected by the officers of the Council;

(d) three clerks in Holy Orders (of whom two shall be persons ordinarily resident in the Province of Canterbury and one shall be ordinarily resident in the Province of York) shall be elected by the General Synod;

(e) six persons [being members of a Diocesan Board of Finance appointed or elected in such manner as the General Synod may from time to time by resolution provide];

(f) three other persons shall be appointed by the Council."

# PART III
## General provisions

Interpretation.  12  (1) In this Measure -

"appointed day" means such day as the Archbishops of Canterbury and York may jointly appoint;

"the Bishoprics Committee" means the committee appointed under section 10 above;

"the Council" means the National Council of the Church of England established by section 1 above;

"executive chairman" means an executive chairman appointed under section 3 above;

"functions" includes powers and duties;

"officer" includes servant;

"the Secretary General" means the Secretary General of the Council;

"year" means the financial year of the Church Commissioners.

(2) References in this Measure to the House of Bishops, the House of Clergy or the House of Laity shall be construed as references to the relevant House of the General Synod.

(3) Except in the context of any specific amendment of any Act or Measure made by this Measure references in any [Act or] Measure (other than this Measure) or in any statutory instrument to the Church Commissioners shall be construed as references to the Council.

(4) References in any Act or Measure (other than this Measure) or in any statutory instrument to the Standing Committee of the General Synod or the Central Board of Finance shall be construed as references to the Council.

|  |  |
|---|---|
| Transitional provisions. | 13 The transitional provisions in Schedule 2 to this Measure shall have effect. |

|  |  |
|---|---|
| Amendments and repeals. | 14 (1) The amendments specified in Schedule 3 to this Measure shall have effect subject to the amendments specified in that Schedule, being minor amendments or amendments consequential on the provisions of this Measure. |

(2) The enactments specified in Schedule 4 to this Measure are hereby repealed to the extent specified in the third column of that Schedule.

|  |  |
|---|---|
| Citation and extent. | 15 (1) This Measure may be cited as the Church of England (Central Institutions) Measure 199-. |

(2) This Measure shall extend to the whole of the provinces of Canterbury and York except the Channel Islands and the Isle of Man.

## SCHEDULE 1 Section 2(3)

# THE NATIONAL COUNCIL
## Constitution and membership

1   The Council shall be a body corporate, with perpetual succession and a common seal.

2   (1) Subject to the following provisions of this Schedule, a member of the Council shall hold and vacate office in accordance with the terms of his appointment.

   (2) Each of the executive chairmen shall serve as such for such number of years, being not less than three and not more than five, as may be determined by the General Synod.

3   A member of the Council may, by notice in writing addressed to the Archbishop of Canterbury, resign his membership.

4   A member of the Council who ceases to be a member shall be eligible for re-appointment: provided that an executive chairman shall be eligible for re-appointment as such for one further period of office only.

5   A member of the Council appointed under section 2(2) above shall, if not otherwise a member of the General Synod, be an *ex officio* member:

   (a)  in the case of a bishop, of the House of Bishops;

   (b)  in the case of any other clerk in Holy Orders, of the House of Clergy; and

   (c)  in the case of a lay person, of the House of Laity.

## Proceedings

6   (1) The quorum of the Council shall be five; and the arrangements relating to meetings of the Council shall be such as the Council may determine.

(2) Subject to paragraph (1) above, the Council shall have power to regulate its own procedure.

7    The validity of any proceedings of the Council shall not be affected by any vacancy among the members or by any defect in the appointment of any member.

8    In the absence of both Archbishops the Council shall elect one of its members to act as chairman.

9    The application of the seal of the Council shall be authenticated by the signature of the Secretary General or of some other person authorised by the Council, either generally or specifically, to act for that purpose.

10   Any document purporting to be a document duly executed under the seal of the Council, or to be signed on behalf of the Council, shall be received in evidence and shall, unless the contrary is proved, be deemed to be so executed or, as the case may be, signed.

## Incidental powers

11   (1)  It shall be within the capacity of the Council as a statutory corporation to do all such things and enter into all such transactions as are incidental or conducive to the discharge of its functions.

     (2)  Without prejudice to the foregoing, the powers of the Council shall include power to acquire or dispose of any property.

## Staff

12   (1)  The Council shall appoint a chief executive, to be known as "the Secretary General", and may appoint such other officers as it may determine.

     (2)  The Council may pay to its officers such remuneration and allowances as it may determine.

     (3)  The Council shall, in the case of such officers as it may determine, pay such pensions, allowances or gratuities to or in respect of them as may be so determined, make such payments towards the provision of such pensions, allowances or gratuities as may be so determined or provide

and maintain such schemes (whether contributory or not) for the payment of such pensions, allowances or gratuities as may be so determined.

13 Where a person enters the employment of the Council on the appointed day having been, immediately before that day, employed by the Church Commissioners, the Central Board of Finance or the Pensions Board, then for the purposes of the Employment Protection (Consolidation) Act 1978 any period during which he was so employed before that day shall count as a period of employment with the Council, and the change of employer shall not break the continuity of the period of employment.

14 It shall be the duty of the officers of the Council, as and when requested by the Council, to assist the Church Commissioners and their committees, the Pensions Board and the Bishoprics Committee in the performance of their functions.

## SCHEDULE 2   Section 13
## TRANSITIONAL PROVISIONS

[to be considered at a later date]

## SCHEDULE 3   Section 14(1)
## MINOR AND CONSEQUENTIAL AMENDMENTS

[to be considered at a later date]

## SCHEDULE 4   Section 14(2)
## REPEALS

[to be considered at a later date]

# Appendix C

# Possible supporting structure of the National Council

## The National Office of the Church of England

C.1    This appendix contains some suggestions about the structure which might support the proposed Council. We believe they provide a sensible basis on which to build. We emphasise again, however, that it would be for the Council to decide on the shape of the organisation to support each of its important tasks. It might wish to take independent professional advice, but it must have the freedom and authority to order its own business as it thinks fit and to decide what its staff should do.

C.2    The responsibilities of the Council could be grouped into four main areas:

- resources for ministry
- mission resources
- heritage and legal services
- finance.

Subject to the different arrangements which might be made in relation to the statutory and other bodies which deal with Church buildings, described further below, each of these areas would be overseen by a part-time executive chairman with a seat on the Council. The Council, in consultation with the relevant chairman, would draw together a committee or board to advise on and support each area of work, and the work itself would be managed by a staff director. Issues of policy and resources would come under the overall direction of the Council. Within its strategic policy, the four chairmen would each lead in their own area of work, both in public and within the Council. They would contribute to the Council's decisions on strategic policy and would take the decisions necessary to implement them within their own areas of responsibility. They would draw on the advice of their own committees. We have looked in some detail at how such committees might be composed and are satisfied that various interests could properly be taken into account with a membership of fewer than 20 on each committee. The Council and the chairmen would have the flexibility to handle different issues in different ways. The single staff service would provide the executive management to advise them and to carry out their decisions.

# Resources for ministry

C.3    The people of God are the Church's primary resource. Under the executive chairman responsible for resources for ministry and his or her committee, a resources for ministry department (RMD) would bring together the Council's responsibilities for different aspects of ministry, ordained and lay, which are at present located in:

- the Advisory Board of Ministry (including the Central Readers' Council)

- the Board of Education (including adult education)

- the Church Commissioners (e.g. issues relating to the Pastoral Measure, stipends policy (the Central Stipends Authority), and clergy housing)

- Archbishops' Officers (principally the Clergy Appointments Adviser)

- the Hospital Chaplaincies Council

- the Pensions Board's administrative responsibilities.

All their functions would become functions of the Council under the leadership of the Archbishops. It would be for the Council and the resources for ministry chairman to decide how they should be carried out and what committee or other structures – if any – would be appropriate to support them.

C.4    The resources for ministry chairman would be responsible to the Council for developing a strategic view of the Church's human resources for ministry. He or she would report regularly to the Council so that trends and developments could be recognised as they emerged and broad policy implications could be identified and directed. The Council would determine the overall direction of new developments where primary legislation or other major changes would result, and would ensure that these were taken to the House of Bishops or General Synod within the strategy developed by the Council. It would also determine if the money was likely to be available.

C.5    Under the overall direction of the Council and the resources for ministry executive chairman the RMD's responsibilities would cover two broad areas:

- the selection, training, and other processes associated with formal authorisation of ministers (ordained and lay). In these areas it would be responsible under the direction of the Council to the

House of Bishops, but with a recognition of General Synod's proper concerns

- the administration of ministry matters. In this it would be responsible under the direction of the Council to General Synod, but with a recognition of the bishop's responsibility for oversight and care of ministry within his diocese.

C.6    Under the overall direction of the Council, and within its strategic policy, the RMD would be responsible to the House of Bishops for managing the national policies of the Church in respect of vocation to, and selection and training for all kinds of episcopally authorised ministry, lay and ordained. (Responsibility for servicing the conduct of bishops' inspections of theological colleges and courses would rest with the secretariat of the House of Bishops.) It would manage the national policies of the Church in respect of strategic planning for the ministry, for the development of suitable patterns of ministry and for clergy conditions of service. It would administer those funds made available by the General Synod for ministerial training, and any other nationally provided ministerial services (except the provision or payment of stipends).

C.7    The RMD would carry out the day to day responsibilities for pensioners which are to be transferred to the Council. Those responsibilities relate to the actual payment of pensions and other payments to individuals, the operation of the CHARM scheme for the housing of retired clergy and the provision and management of residential and nursing homes.

## Mission resources

C.8    The mission resources function of the Council would plan the mission of the Church in its widest sense and ensure the effective use and co-ordination of the resources for mission of the Church at national level. The mission resources chairman would take the lead responsibility, under the overall direction of the Council, for the work of:

- the Board of Mission

- the Board for Christian Unity (currently the Council for Christian Unity)

- the Board of Education

- the Board for Social Responsibility

and would also take on the responsibility for oversight of work in Urban Priority Areas and on Black Anglican Concerns at present located in the

General Synod Office. The mission resources chairman and his or her committee and staff director would undertake the oversight and co-ordinating functions in respect of these bodies which is at present undertaken by the Policy Committee of the Standing Committee of the General Synod, helping them to determine priorities and dealing with questions affecting more than one Board.

C.9    The four Boards would, under the mission resources committee and its executive chairman, serve and support the Council in discharging its functions and would report as necessary to the General Synod under the direction of the Council. Initially, the responsibilities of the four Boards could remain largely as at present, except that adult education for formal lay ministry could move from the Board of Education to the new resources for ministry department. Against the background of all the other change in progress it would not be sensible to propose the wholesale reorganisation of these Boards, or to seek to impose a single organisational model on such diverse areas of work. There is, however, considerable scope for the Council to review what work is done in each Board, and how, and for further reducing the size and number of their various committees. The points we make elsewhere in our report about simplifying structures and improving styles of work apply to the Boards as to other parts of the proposed national organisation.

# Heritage and legal services

C.10    This part of the sub-structure would embrace various aspects of the Council's responsibilities – for the national policy of the Church in respect of its buildings, for the provision of its central legal services and for the operation of certain appellate functions – which are presently scattered among the Church Commissioners, the General Synod Office and various other Church-related bodies. That should enable greater attention to be given to important activities which are in some cases at present inadequately co-ordinated and resourced.

*Buildings and heritage*

C.11    The Church of England has nearly 16,400 church buildings, of which nearly 13,000 are listed. Some 40% of the Grade 1 listed buildings in the country are in the Church's ownership. In 1992, the Church spent some £112 million on the repair and maintenance of its buildings, only £10.4 million of which came from the Government in the form of grants.

C.12   Several different bodies are at present responsible for different aspects of the Church's interest in the built heritage. Some of them have a statutory basis. They include:

- the Council for the Care of Churches (CCC)

- the Cathedrals Fabric Commission for England (CFCE)

- the Advisory Board for Redundant Churches (ABRC)

- the Redundant Churches Committee (RCC) of the Church Commissioners

- the Churches Conservation Trust (CCT), a joint Church/State body.

Their responsibilities are co-ordinated through occasional meetings of the officers of the bodies, the General Synod's Working Party on State Aid and the office of the Secretary-General (for example, in relation to negotiations with the Department of National Heritage on the Ecclesiastical Exemption). The work of the Church Commissioners also brings together the ABRC, the RCC and the CCT.

C.13   Although the various bodies draw their specific remit from their respective statutes or other founding document, they are all, in the broader sense, established within the context of a wider understanding or concordat on heritage matters between the Government (including English Heritage), Parliament and the Church. A means is needed by which the Church can define and develop policy across the range of heritage issues, and relate its buildings to its mission; the Council would provide the mechanism for this.

C.14   The Council could establish a **Church Heritage Board** with the following functions:

- to secure the development and implementation of policies to encourage the optimum use of the Church's buildings and related resources in furthering its mission and in the effective discharge of the Church's responsibilities towards the national heritage

- to negotiate with the Government, English Heritage, Parliament and other relevant bodies on heritage matters within a framework of policy set by the Council and endorsed by the General Synod

- to act as a central point of contact on Church heritage matters and to present a clear corporate stance to Government and the public on the Church's heritage responsibilities

- to encourage the closest practicable working between the various Church heritage bodies and to ensure the most effective deployment of national resources in support of the Church's heritage work.

C.15　The membership of the board would include the chairmen and chief executive officers of the various Church heritage bodies and representatives of other bodies with a substantial interest in Church heritage matters (such as the Association of English Cathedrals and the Ecclesiastical Judges Association). It would be chaired by the Council's heritage and legal services chairman and serviced by a staff member with the task of co-ordinating the work of the staff of the various Church heritage advisory bodies. The Board would replace the present Working Party on State Aid.

C.16　It would not be sensible to move immediately to merge all the Church heritage bodies into one. Several of the bodies were examined in a recent review, *The Care of Redundant Churches* (HMSO 1990). Unscrambling the present statutory basis of the organisations would be difficult and in some cases involve renegotiating understandings reached over a lengthy period with the Government. Nevertheless the Council should undertake a re-examination of all these bodies when the new Church Heritage Board has been working for some time, and a much earlier re-examination of their functions where these overlap.

*Legal services*

C.17　It could be more effective and economical if the separate legal staff of the Church's national institutions were brought together in one department under a legal services director who would attend meetings of the Council and be answerable to the Council. They would form part of the single central staff of the Council and would be available to all parts of the central structure. A senior lawyer would be specifically assigned to the General Synod to act as its legal adviser. He or she would serve the Synod independently and would be responsible for providing legal advice when the Synod was in session, for elections to the Synod and internal elections, and for the running of revision committees. We suggest that the heritage and legal services chairman supported by the director should have a major responsibility for pursuing the revision and simplification of the ecclesiastical law, with all the potential for administrative and other savings at all levels of the Church which this would allow.

149

# Finance

C.18 As with its resources of people and buildings, so the Church needs a body at national level to oversee its resources of money. We envisage that the Council would delegate significant responsibilities to its **finance committee**, led by an executive chairman who would be a member of the Council and charged with directing, under the oversight of the Council, the national financial policies of the Church. The membership of the committee should include clear representation from the dioceses (who in future would play an even more important role than hitherto in the Church's overall financing) along with other people of proven financial skill and ability.

C.19 The **functions** of the finance department, under the finance committee and its executive chairman, would include:

- developing an overview of the Church's finances and preparing financial plans for presentation to the Council

- preparing the budget for national Church responsibilities

- providing such central services (such as clergy payroll administration) as the dioceses wished

- managing (and simplifying, where appropriate) the overall financial flows within the Church

- monitoring the financial position of the Church as recorded in diocesan and parochial accounts and seeking to provide help in emergencies

- overseeing the production and use of Church statistics

- providing central support for stewardship initiatives and otherwise actively promoting the income of the Church

- promoting and overseeing fundraising initiatives

- overseeing certain trust, property and investment interests

- advising the Council on the financial implications of policy proposals

- monitoring the central financial systems and taking responsibility for their probity and efficiency

- developing and co-ordinating an information technology and telecommunications strategy across the whole Church.

The finance department would provide advice and support to all the other departments, the Council itself and its committees.

# Central secretariat

C.20   The servicing of the Council itself, of the House of Bishops and of the various Commissions of the Synod (such as the Liturgical Commission) would be the responsibility of a central secretariat. This would take on all the remaining responsibilities at present undertaken by the General Synod Office, except for its functions in respect of servicing the Synod and its Business and Appointments Committees; overseeing elections to the Synod; and servicing legislative and liturgical business going through the Synod. These functions would in future be the responsibility of a much smaller Synod secretariat acting under a Clerk of the Synod (see paragraph 6.38). The important central personnel function, including training and development, as well as the provision of staff and accommodation, staff welfare and determination of staff conditions of service, could come under the auspices of the central secretariat (or the finance department).

# Communications and publishing

C.21   The Council would have as one of its core tasks promoting the mission of the Church through effective communication. It would be responsible for ensuring the consistent presentation of the Church's message, and of the particular policies through which at any one time it sought to enhance the effectiveness of the Church's mission and ministry. More effective communication with dioceses and parishes would be a prime aim. The Council might wish to appoint a director of communications to be responsible for ensuring that the Council adopted a strategic approach to this end, and that all parts of the national organisation actively promoted the Council's communications policies. The aim would not be the adoption of a single line which sought to muzzle dissent but to ensure that all parts of the Church accepted their share in the responsibility for improving communications both within the Church and to those outside its immediately active membership.

C.22   All the present communications staffs should, like all other staff at the national level, become part of the single staff service, and act as a single communications staff to serve the national level of the Church. In view of the demands upon him, the Archbishop of Canterbury would continue to be served by his own press officer, who would work very closely, as now, with the rest of the Church's communications staff. The development of such a staff should enable the more effective deployment of resources and possibly achieve some saving on their present level.

C.23 The publishing activities of Church House (which also serve the National Society) are presently separate from the rest of the communications operation there. It would strengthen the coherent and forceful presentation of the Church's message if these two activities were in future brought together under the overall leadership of the Council's director of communications, while leaving a good deal of commercial freedom to the publishing manager and his or her colleagues.